APPETIZINGLY YOURS

Employee Share Ownership Plans

Employee Share Ownership Plans

Perry Phillips

John Wiley & Sons Canada, Ltd
Toronto • New York • Chichester • Weinheim • Brisbane • Singapore

John Wiley & Sons Canada Ltd
22 Worcester Road
Etobicoke, Ontario
M9W 1L1

National Library of Canada Cataloguing in Publication Data

Phillips, Perry, 1951-
    Employee share ownership plans

Includes index.
ISBN 0-471-64622-9

1. Employee stock options. 2. Employee ownership. I. Title.
HD4928.S74P44 2001   658.3'225   C2001-930433-1

Production Credits

Cover: Interrobang Graphic Design Inc.
Text Design: Ian J. Koo
Printer: Tri-Graphic Printing

C O N T E N T S

ESOPs in Canada

EMPLOYEE OWNERSHIP HAS ALWAYS SEEMED to me like an idea just waiting to blossom forth in Canada. My personal and business trips to Canada have always left an impression of a country that has a strong sense of community and mutual obligation (stronger than the U.S., I must sadly say). Sharing ownership with employees just seems like a natural fit, a way to combine the market capitalism of the economy with the social goals of the society. Yet it has always been the U.S. that has taken the lead on this issue, largely for idiosyncratic reasons.

In the 1970s, Louis Kelso, a San Francisco investment banker and attorney, met with Russell Long, chair of the powerful Senate Finance Committee. Kelso had long been on a crusade to promote the idea of "ESOPs" (employee stock ownership plans) as a way to make the capitalist system both fairer and more efficient. Kelso thought capitalism was a wonderful idea—there just weren't enough capitalists. Real wealth he argued, could only come through ownership, not wages, which he correctly predicted would stagnate as technology and capital investments grew in the latter art of the twentieth century. But workers could not become capitalists because, of course, they lacked capital. The solution would be to have their employer use its assets as collateral to borrow money to buy ownership for them, repaying it out of the future (and, Kelso hoped to convince Long, tax-deductible) earnings of the company. Employers would get a tax break, workers would get ownership, and corporate performance would improve because workers now had a reason to care about profits. So, in the end, shareholders would do well too. So would the country, because more people would have more money to invest and make purchases, and there would be less strain on the government from demands to redistribute wealth through the tax system.

This singular notion of combining Adam Smith and Karl Marx appealed mightily to Long, a conservative Democrat with some populist strains. Long convinced his colleagues to go along with the tax breaks, and, in 1974, ESOPs were created. In the ensuing 26 years, 11,000 plans have been created, covering over 8.5 million employees. By the early 1990s, companies that may not have liked the mechanics of ESOPs had become convinced that employee ownership really did work and started to share ownership in other ways, such as giving everyone stock options or through stock purchase plans with impressive discounts. By the turn of the century, over 25 million employees (23 per cent of the private sector work force) owned stock in their company in one way or another. Studies showed that employee ownership companies did indeed generally outperform their competitors and employees often accumulated significant wealth they would never have otherwise dreamed possible.

As Perry Phillips points out in this much needed book, employee ownership in Canada has not had the good fortune of having a Russell Long to shepherd the idea through Parliament. Lacking the federal tax framework to make the idea more appealing, Canadian companies have relied instead on some favorable provincial legislation, tweaking stock option laws, and providing ownership even in the absence of any tax breaks. To be sure, tax incentives are great to have, but the U.S. experience shows that the tax benefits are easily outweighed by the performance, planning, and, for many companies, ethical or community benefits. Offering ownership is also becoming increasingly imperative in Canada and the U.S. just to attract and retain good people, especially in the technology sector.

This book will help Canadian companies steer through the alternatives they have in creating the most efficient plan possible. It couldn't have a more appropriate author. Perry Phillips has worked in the employee ownership field longer than anyone I know in Canada and truly is a national resource on the idea. His expertise has been combined with a generous commitment of time to help promote the idea through the ESOP Association (Canada), which he started, and his active involvement in a variety of other forums throughout Canada and the U.S. I look forward to referring our Canadian friends to this new book.

Corey Rosen
Executive Director
National Center for Employee Ownership
Oakland, California

A C K N O W L E D G E M E N T S

EMPLOYEE SHARE OWNERSHIP ENCOMPASSES many disciplines. This book could not have been written without the contributions of the following experts in their fields.

In Pre-ESOP Issues, Michael Fremes, CA, wrote the chapter on ESOPs and income tax, and Harvey Wortsman, LLB, wrote the chapter on ESOPs and legal issues.

These were first presented at the annual Canadian Tax Foundation's Corporate Tax Management Conference in 1999, and was therefore included in the Foundation's publication Corporate Tax Management Conference 1999: R&D Credits Today, Innovation Tomorrow, as "ESOPs: Income Tax Implications" and "Legal Requirements and Implications of ESOPs and Stock Options" respectively.

In Post-ESOP Issues, Dave Tyson wrote on profit-sharing and Danny Grieg wrote about open-book management, both in Chapter 9. In Chapter 10, Jerry Kalish wrote about ESOPs in the US.

I thank these contributors and advise the reader that any errors or omissions in this book are mine and mine alone.

I would like to thank Ron Edwards, Focus Strategic Communications, for providing in the course of his diligent editing of the first draft, the most polite constructive criticism I have ever encountered; Elizabeth McCurdy, assistant editor, John Wiley & Sons Canada, Ltd, for her patience and care for us; and Karen Milner, Editor, for believing in the project and shepherding it through multiple business obstacles. Thanks to Susan Yates, my agent; to Kathleen Crowley, for keeping me on track to completion; to Sue Hamilton, who, because of her incredible ability to understand my dictation, typed virtually the whole manuscript from cassettes; and to Sue Anderson for her cheerful help at deadline time.

I thank my fellow shareowner Ian McDowell who helped with the research and held the fort while I worked on the book.

Thanks to my wife Helen Phillips for working the second shift on this project, and to our daughter Joanna. Without their support and love this book would not exist.

Dedicated to Joanna Phillips,
with the hope that this book will do some small good in the grown-up
world in which she will, soon enough, assume her place.

INTRODUCTION

IN SILICON VALLEY where secretaries and shippers, technology gurus and marketing wizards trade their time and talents for shares in the company in hopes of a big payoff, it is fashionable to refer to their contract as "The Golden Handcuff." "Golden Handcuffs" is a term that's used by the media and industry to indicate the compensation schemes offered to keep key executives in a company and to attract new executives to the company. The schemes present exceptional rewards based on the results of future growth and value of the company. And the so-called handcuff has paid off handsomely for many as their companies have had explosive growth and been bought out or gone public. Certainly we're all aware of the many millionaires created by Microsoft and many of the high technology companies. However, there is a large number of old economy companies that have implemented plans that have produced a substantial number of millionaires both in Canada and the United States.

These success stories have brought welcome attention to a workplace solution whose time has come—employee share ownership plans (ESOPs). However the golden handcuff doesn't truly represent what ESOPs are all about.

For the past decade, my passion and practice has been the design and implementation of ESOPs for award-winning Canadian and American businesses. A traditional ESOP is more balanced than golden handcuffs. It is typically a long-term strategy and has greater flexibility than the golden handcuffs, which is based solely upon a specific target. A well-designed ESOP is designed to keep the "gold" and drop the "handcuffs." Here then are the factors fundamental to all ESOPs:

• Help attract and retain key employees

• Create an ownership mentality because employees are owners

• Recognize and value the contributions of all employees

• Boost productivity and competitiveness

• Give employees a chance to share in the company's success

As President of ESOP Builders Inc. and one of the founding directors of the ESOP Association of Canada, I have presented briefs to international conferences on ESOPs, the Canadian Tax Foundation, and the Canadian Institute of Chartered Accountants. I have met with federal Ministers of Finance and other members of parliament to encourage changes to our tax laws that would in turn encourage more companies to implement ESOPs. Our highly skilled work force is our last great natural resource and if we fail to take steps to protect it, Canada will be left behind in this new global economy. The so-called brain drain already has had dramatic effects on not only the high tech industry but also on companies that require special skills to produce their goods and services.

In addition to the number of practical reasons to embrace ESOPs, you'll read about important philosophical reasons as well. For example, ESOPs

• Represent a new way of thinking for an interdependent economy

• Gel with these times of unprecedented and broad-based stock ownership

• Represent a real way to narrow the widening wage gap

• Provide an opportunity for capital gain for retirement

This book outlines the processes that are the foundation of an ESOP and some of the nuances that make a plan come alive. It includes case studies and a comprehensive resource directory for more information.

Whether you're looking to attract and retain skilled workers, creating a succession plan for a family business, want to recognize the contributions your employees have made to the company's success, or need a method to turn a company around through productivity and morale improvements, read this book. ESOPs present a win-win solution in a world in which it is no longer business as usual.

Within the last 20 years the world has seen an explosion of new ideas, new technologies, and new advances in just about every field of human endeavour. Knowledge is said to be doubling every five years— even sooner in some areas of scientific research. How can we actualize our sophisticated systems and increasing knowledge for the good of our society as well as for the good of our country? If we are to harness the abilities and the potential of Canadians in the workplace, we require breakthroughs in methodologies that utilize assets that have been previously underutilized. As shown in the United States, the United Kingdom, and many countries around the world over the last 25 years, a major breakthrough has been made through the use of employee share ownership plans. Through these plans we can work together to harness the benefits of all the new technologies and new ideas coming forth at this point in time.

One reason ESOPs started in the United States was to address the widening gap between the middle class and the wealthy. Studies have shown that the top 1 per cent of people in the United States owned approximately 80 per cent of the wealth, and it was felt that a continuation of this process would, in effect, be the end of democracy in the United States.

Individuals can create wealth two ways. The first is through their own work effort; however, there are only 24 hours in a day, personal and labour can contribute only so much to a person's income. The second method is capital accumulation: the ownership of capital assets that may increase in value without the input of a person's individual labour component. Unfortunately, many people do not have the knowledge, skill, or opportunity to participate in the capital asset growth of a company. ESOPs address this issue by insuring that all employees will benefit by ownership in the companies they work for. This has tremendous implications not only on the individual employees but also on the political and social fabric of the nation. A wealthier middle class has tremendous implications on many issues in our current economy. It means less reliance upon governments for future pensions. It means a bigger source of income taxes that can be used to help the poor in our society. It means people are more able to take control of their own destinies to attain their specific goals in life.

In times of economic expansion crime rates go down, and in times of economic recession crime rates increase. Would we not be better off as a society to increase the wealth of as many people as possible? Wealth cannot be created by governments; wealth is created by the labour of the workforce. If the employees get the benefits of their work through ownership in their companies, wealth is spread without an intervention mechanism such as higher income taxes. Of course not all people want to give empowerment to the employees. Some people believe that if Canadian employees begin to control their own destinies, governments will have a smaller role in monitoring and creating laws to restrict and focus the allocation of assets within society. I agree that there are winners and losers in implementing ESOPs. The clear winners are the employees who are now able to benefit from another source of income. This income increases potential for wealth and the ability to control one's own destiny, meaning that employees won't have to rely upon unions, government, or any institutional setting that seeks to control and dictate what their lives should be.

The losers on the other hand are the large institutions that will start to lose control over the very people that keep them in their positions of power. Looking again to the United States, both the Republicans and the Democrats have put into place a very sophisticated level of ESOP legislation, which supports the concept that individuals should have control over their own destiny. Republicans regard ESOPs as a means of empowering individuals, whereas the Democrats see ESOPs as a means of spreading wealth. ESOPs do both, and it is important for Canadians to realize that if we are to compete in the future against countries that have many times our population base and much lower unit costs, we have to utilize our greatest skill: the ability of our people to innovate and create new ways of doing business.

In this book I will show that ESOPs are effective and do create productivity levels that are necessary for Canadian companies to compete in a global marketplace. However, this is not enough. For breadwinners, no price can be put on the knowledge that their hard work has not only improved their family's life but also created something that is bigger than themselves. They are creating a successful company that will, in the long term, help them to achieve personal and financial goals. This approach has been proven in many countries. In the United States for the last 25 years, in Britain over the last 10 years, and in countries such as Germany, Spain, France, and developing countries, companies are starting to look at implementing ESOPs as a means of increasing the wealth of their people.

Not all private or public companies are suitable for ESOPs. Research in the United States indicates that approximately 25 per cent of companies appear to have the suitable cultural and structural supports to implement an ESOP. However, given that figure, very few companies have actually developed an ESOP plan to both help their employees and the company grow. I believe that Canadian companies must utilize some type of ESOP program if we are to remain competitive on the world stage.

This book was written for those owners and employees who realize that there is no limit to what can be achieved by a team of dedicated individuals. These are the people that can utilize and benefit substantially from an ESOP within their corporation.

To achieve a successful ESOP, it is important to have access to knowledgeable professionals in the area. An ESOP entails many different aspects such as design, communication, law, tax, and valuation, and one consultant alone connot serve them all. In appendix 9 you will find a list of professional firms and associations. While this is by no means an all-inclusive or exhaustive list, it may help the reader to at least begin their search.

HOW TO USE THIS BOOK

This book has been written for readers who are interested in learning about the design and implementation of employee share ownership plans. It addresses three types of readers. The first are business owners of privately held companies who wish to sell or transfer equity to employees. The second type is the stakeholders of publicly held companies, both senior executives and their employees. The third type are professional advisors such as accountants, lawyers, tax advisors, and financial planners who want to help clients in implementing and designing employee share ownership plans.

To meet the needs of each group of readers, the book deals with Pre-ESOP issues and Post-ESOP issues. Pre-ESOP issues include ESOP planning, design, and implementation. Pre-ESOP issues also include the period of time during which the ESOP is implemented into the corporate culture of the company. These pre-ESOP processes can take anywhere from three to six months to complete. In many cases in which we have been involved, the idea for the ESOP has been proposed either by the business owners or by the employees as much as three years prior to the time that a designer was brought in to help implement a plan.

For business owners, or for someone who is considering putting an ESOP plan into place, I suggest starting with Chapter 2, ESOP Objectives. The chapter explains the types of candidates who would likely succeed at this type of process, and the process itself, which is key to implementing a successful ESOP. Continue to Chapter 3, Designing ESOPs, which goes into the detail of designing an ESOP and addresses a lot of the issues involved in the administration, communication, and troubleshooting that occurs when putting an ESOP into place in a privately held company. These two chapters, along with the Appendices outlining the types of plans and the appropriate forms, and the communication pieces needed to set the process in motion, will likely suffice for most readers who are interested in starting the process immediately. Chapters 4 to 7 deal with detailed technical issues around financing, business valuation, income taxes, and legal matters, and although these are important, the business owner must simply understand some of the technical issues to converse knowledgeably with professionals when implementing the design of the ESOP.

For the stakeholders of publicly held companies, both senior executives and employees, many of the pre-ESOP issues in the earlier chapters are not as important as the post-ESOP issues addressed in Chapters 9 and 10. These chapters address the issues relevant to ESOPs for those public companies that have some type of shareholder plan already in place. These issues include profit sharing, the use of open book management, and implementation and proper use of cross-border ESOPs. For the business owners and employees of privately held companies, once the ESOP is in place post-ESOP issues occur, usually six months to a year after the ESOP is set-up. Chapters 9 and 10 provide useful information for business owners to understand what issues will be coming down the road, in order to start planning now.

For the third group of readers, professional advisors, a knowledge of the process is critical for the success of an ESOP. For those readers we suggest Chapters 1 through 3, which deal with the communication, design, and implementation of the ESOP.

What is an ESOP?

IN TECHNICAL TERMS, an ESOP is a formal stock equity plan that can include stock equity, stock options, or phantom stock. The definitions for these terms will be provided later in the chapter. An ESOP can be part of an employee benefits package or a corporate financing strategy. The plan can be open to key personnel or all employees, enabling them to purchase in total from 1 per cent to 100 per cent ownership in the company with the securities acquired through cash payment, profit sharing, bonuses, or services rendered. The equity ownership allows qualifying employees to participate in and benefit from the growth of the company in return for a commitment to stay for the long haul. ESOPs allow employee-owners to share in the company's success through increased share value that can be sheltered for tax-free gain. Favourable tax treatment is available because these gains can be classified not as income earned, but as a capital gain, which is taxed at a much lower rate than income.

That is the technical description. In fact, ESOPs defy easy explanation; every plan is unique. The plan's purpose, participation, and parameters are flexible and tailored to the individual company. In general, though, there are certain common results. When coupled with a corporate philosophy of participative management, ESOPs create an ownership mentality. Employees think and act like owners because they actually are owners. Workplace dynamics shift from a "working for" to a "working with" mentality. The outcomes are improved motivation, communication, productivity, and profitability.

THE THREE TYPES OF ESOP

ESOPs are built with three basic tools: stock equity, stock options, or phantom stock units. A plan may comprise only one, a combination of any two, or all three tools.

Stock Equity

Stock equity is the legal transfer of ownership of a share of stock issued by a company. An employee who owns this share has ownership that may or may not have additional rights attached to it. For example, the share may allow the employee to vote at the annual shareholder's meeting, or the share may be non-voting. Stock equity has the greatest potential for creating an ownership mentality within the company because the employee generally has to pay for the stock. This payment requires the employee to take an investment risk in the company. It is this risk potential that puts the original owners and the new employee owners on the same level.

Stock Options

Stock options constitute a contract between the company and the employee to sell equity to the employee at some point in the future, at a price calculated in the present day. At that future date, if the company has increased in value, the employee will be able to purchase company stock at a significant discount and have a real gain in wealth. If the share value declines, the employee does not lose anything because he or she simply does not exercise the option to buy the stock. A stock option can be a motivator and a surrogate for ownership. However, it may not be effective as equity ownership.

Phantom Stock

Phantom stock units mirror real stock equity with equivalent rights—except the right to vote. There is, however, no legal transfer of ownership, and this tends to be the greatest drawback of phantom stock. It does not create the conditions necessary for true ownership because the employee does not have legal title to any of the assets of the company. However, by adding equity conversion rights to these units—in effect a super bonus scheme—phantom stock can approach true equity plans. The equity conversion allows the phantom units to be converted to real stock equity upon a liquidity event. For example, five years from the time that the phantom plan is put into place, an outside purchaser may buy shares of the company. Employees with the phantom stock units can transfer their units into real shares of the company prior to the closing of the acquisition, sell those shares to the acquirer, and realize a substantial gain in equity. Phantom stock units are used when the ownership group is not comfortable with transferring real equity ownership to the employees and does not want employees to have a vote.

The term "phantom plans" is used by practitioners in the field but not when presenting to employees, because the term tends to indicate something false. To avoid this problem, many phantom plans are known as either participation or value-added plans.

THE IMPORTANCE OF EQUITY TYPES

Stock equity, stock options, and phantom stock may be viewed as a continuum, with stock plans being on the extreme left, stock options in the middle, and phantom plans on the extreme right. The left portion of this continuum represents the maximum changed mindset with regards to employee ownership mentality. In other words, when employees actually own shares in a company, they believe that they are owners, and the process of participation is easier to implement. Participative management in ESOPs will be discussed in Chapter 8: Administration and Communication.

In the middle of the continuum, stock options are less effective in creating an ownership mentality due to the fact that the employee does not actually own anything. He or she merely has the right to future ownership. This right can still be a powerful force in creating an ownership mentality, but it is not as strong as pure equity ownership.

On the extreme right of the continnum are phantom plans. These have limited ability to create an ownership mentality as there is no ownership nor is there likely to be. However, with certain conditions attached to these plans, some ownership mentality can be created. In fact, these plans are still better than no plan at all. In many cases a phantom plan can be a precursor to a share equity or option plan at some future date.

Why do some companies use only one type of plan while others mix and match the elements? The answer lies in the culture of the company and the mindset of the current ownership group. A culture of open sharing of information, for example, will likely go for an equity and/or option plan, while a culture that is secretive will probably favor the phantom plan. There is no right or wrong approach to this design issue. Each plan must meet the criteria as set by both the culture and ownership group's comfort level in terms of sharing ownership. The key to a successful plan is proper identification of the culture and ownership type at the beginning of the assignment so as to create a match. Another aspect that can come into play in choosing the plan type is whether or not the company can legally offer equity and/or option plans. For example, accounting and legal firms may not be able to issue shares and thus have to look at a phantom plan augmented by some participative designs to achieve a successful ESOP.

So first determine your company's culture. For example, if your company tends to give out quarterly financial information, has training programs that encourage employees to understand financial statements, and is open with the communication of these issues, the most effective plan for your company would be a stock equity and/or a stock option plan. If your company is concerned with attracting and keeping your key people only, you may want to look at a pure stock option plan. If your company tends to not communicate its financial positions, does not have a profit-sharing plan, and makes decisions from the top down and not the bottom up, you should probably consider some type of phantom plan to start with.

CONCLUSION

ESOPs go beyond the concept of a golden handcuff, where an employee is chained to the outcome of the company, to one where an employee is motivated to see that the company is a success—through money—for everyone in that company. ESOPs are flexible and may be used in many situations for a variety of purposes. Because of their adaptability, no two ESOPs are the same, and each ESOP may be planned and custom fit to a particular culture and type of company. Whether the company is looking at an ESOP for attraction or retention purposes, or for purposes of succession planning, or for higher productivity and value for the current business owners, it is important to assess whether the company is in fact a good candidate for an ESOP. Because of the expense and the implications of addressing ESOPs and introducing them to an employee group, it is critical that the ownership group determine this as soon as possible.

ESOP Objectives

THERE ARE WELL DOCUMENTED BENEFITS to putting ESOPs in place in companies across all economic sectors. ESOPs address key workplace issues such as productivity, competitiveness, survival, succession, recruiting, and retention. From a more philosophical perspective, ESOPs can help address broader societal issues such as the wage gap and the impending retirement crisis by fostering a climate of inclusive capitalism.

Inclusive capitalism is the means by which a society distributes its wealth on the basis of a fair distribution without the intervention of government or institutional organizations. It is market forces at work allowing the proper spread of increased wealth to all people who are producing that wealth. It is, in effect, the purest form and the highest level of capitalism that can be obtained.

Surveys and outcomes of ESOP implementation in Canada indicate that ESOPs help attract and retain a motivated work force and that they help boost productivity and profitability. Although the samplings are relatively small in Canada, the findings are supported by the American experience. In one Canadian study by ESOP Builders Inc. (a Toronto-based ESOP consulting firm) in 1998, 2,000 small-to medium-size high tech companies were surveyed as to how employers thought employees would react in the following instances. The same questions were asked in an employee survey in the United States in 1993, and the results were fairly similar. For example, in Canada 90 per cent of the owners felt that the employees would be proud to own stock in their company. In the United States 75 per cent of the employees actually said that they were proud to own stock in their company. In terms of retention and attraction, in Canada the employers felt that 82 per cent of the employees would want to stay longer if they owned stock. In the United States 65 per cent actually felt that they would stay longer if they owned stock in a company. These results support the retention and attraction factor of ESOPs.

In terms of productivity, Canadian employers felt that 75 per cent of the employees would work harder at their job because they owned company stock; in the United States 43 per cent of employees felt that they did work harder because they owned company stock. In terms of employee satisfaction, in Canada 65 per cent of employees believed employee ownership made their work more satisfying, while 50 per cent of US employees believed that their work was more satisfying in an ESOP company. In many Canadian companies that have implemented ESOPs, productivity improvements and retention and attraction rates have improved significantly to those companies. One high tech company reduced its employee turnover rate from 30 per cent to 10 per cent after the ESOP was introduced. Another company in a manufacturing field decreased its wasted inventory so much that it increased profitability by over 20 per cent. Many other studies are available online from the National Centre of Employee Ownership. See the end of the book for a list of web sites.

But the mere fact of setting up an ESOP does not automatically transform a corporate culture. It takes more than a shareholder's agreement; employers and employees must embrace the special dynamics of shared ownership and commitment. A shareholder's agreement is simply an agreement between the employees and the owners, setting out the terms and conditions of what it means to be an owner in that particular company. However, when coupled with a corporate philosophy that recognizes the contributions of all workers and stresses participitative management, ESOPs become the winning solution they're designed to be. A participative culture and environment will be discussed more fully in Chapter 8: Administration and Communication.

A CONVERGENCE OF TRENDS

We are in a new economy, one of interdependence through mutually beneficial business relationships. The increasing globalization of commerce and cross-border capital flow are changing the standards for business. As a result, regulatory authorities are working to harmonize accounting and auditing practices to formalize global standards and even out competitive advantages and disadvantages. For example, in the United Kingdom accounting practices allow the write-off of good will upon an acquisition, which gives an advantage to United Kingdom acquirers since they can afford to pay more for a company than a North American company, which cannot write off good will. Clearly, a nation out of step with world standards will ultimately be disadvantaged in business. A clear example of this is the lack of ESOP legislation by Canadian government at the federal level when compared to its major trading competitors such as the United States and the United Kingdom. The explosion of technology is being driven by the trend towards globalization and that explosion has placed a new value on the knowledge-based work force—it is a key national resource that must be protected.

This convergence of trends resulted in ESOPs. The baby boomers are starting to enter their pre-retirement years and seek to balance work and life. At the same time, the generation following the boomers has fewer people and they have a different outlook on work and recreation. In addition to demographic trends and the economic boom, high technology and the shift towards a global economy have opened national borders and allowed people of different cultures and skill sets more access to more work places around the world. The result is employees who are more self reliant and employers who must reward their employees to get them to stay longer. ESOPs are in sync with the world shifting paradigms.

ATTRACTING AND RETAINING MOTIVATED WORKERS

People assets do not appear on the financial statements of a company, but the business cannot operate successfully without attracting and keeping key people. There has been a recent change, however, in the United States and Canada regarding who the key people are in an organization. It used to be that only senior executives were seen as being worthy of special compensation packages in options and in equity programs. However, more progressive companies have identified that all people in an organization are key, from the people who answer the phones at the reception desk, up to and including the chairman of the board. Each has his or her own responsibilities and accountability to improving the value of the company in his or her own area of work within the company. Wendy's, for example, being a fast food chain, put in a stock option plan for all their employees, including the people at the cash register. Normally in the fast food industry, an annual turnover employee rate of 300 per cent is considered reasonable. Wendy's, by putting in their stock option plan, was able to cut their turnover rate to just over 80 per cent.

As we enter the twenty-first century, the demand for key people in all industries has increased throughout the world. Demand is particularly high in the information technology sector.

In December 1998, *Canadian Business* reported that 43,000 Canadians went to the United States to work in 1997, the majority of them in the high tech industries. That was up from 11,000 in 1990. The global need for skilled workers shows no signs of abating. The March 1999 Standard Employer's Report on computer services, noted that the growth of the computing industry is being restricted because of a shortage of skilled labour. The number of positions in the IT field has doubled in the last two years. In 1997, the Information Technology Association of America estimated that there were 346,000 unfilled IT positions. It is estimated that by 2002 there will be over 1 million unfilled IT positions in the United States alone.

ESOP Builders Inc. conducted a recent survey on ESOPs at 1200 high tech companies across Canada; 90 per cent of respondents with ESOPs said the plans had helped attract employees and 75 per cent said they had been a factor in retaining staff.

JOBS IN PRODUCTIVITY AND PROFITABILITY

The Organization for Economic Cooperation and Development (OECD) reports that Canada has had the lowest rate of productivity growth in the G7 group of companies over the last 25 years. Further, it predicts that unless patterns change, Canada's per capita GDP will drop from 10 per cent above the OECD average to 15 per cent below it within 20 years, and the Canadian standard of living will freefall. According to the Centre for the Study of Living Standards, a Canadian worker is 20 per cent less productive than his or her American counterpart. I believe that this difference results from the United States having had a detailed legislated agenda of ESOPs as part of their economic plan for the last 25 years and the fact that one out of five American workers own shares in the companies they work for.

ESOPs can foster a corporate culture where a motivated work force sees the benefit in sharing ideas, trimming costs, and working more productively. According to a 1986 study done by the Toronto Stock Exchange, a comparison of ESOP and non-ESOP public companies showed that ESOP companies had:

- 123 per cent higher five-year profit growth

- 95 per cent higher net profit margin

- 24 per cent greater productivity

- a 2–10 per cent premium on the stock market

- 92.26 per cent higher return on average total equity

- 65.52 per cent higher return on capital

- 31.54 per cent lower debt/equity ratio

US studies over the past 24 years support the TSE findings.

A Toronto-based communications firm established an ESOP to help manage explosive growth. The ESOP has been instrumental in helping the company grow into a multinational firm with a sense of community and an atmosphere of excitement and innovation. Two-thirds of the employees are shareholders and employee satisfaction is at an all-time high.

Another organization has seen a 50 per cent increase in profitability after the implementation of an ESOP. Typical of the new corporate culture, an employee on the manufacturing line who was a shareholder stepped forward and helped find a solution that saved the company $20,000, the equivalent of increasing sales by $200,000.

ESOPs AND SUCCESSION PLANNING

A study of 750 family firms in Canada, conducted by the Deloitte and Touche Centre of Tax Education Research at the University of Waterloo, was reported in *The Globe and Mail* in January 1999. It found that more than half of the heads of family-led companies expected to step down in the next decade. Nearly two-thirds of all companies had no contingency plan regarding the death or disability of their leader. More than half had no succession plan. Close to 70 per cent of respondents were 45 years of age or older and 7 per cent of them were 65 or older. Deloitte and Touche estimates that family businesses account for approximately $1.3 trillion in sales each year in Canada and employ 4.7 million full-time workers and 1.3 million part-time workers.

The question for owners ready to retire is where to sell their assets. For many company owners the best solution is to sell to employees, which is why an ESOP can be the ideal succession plan for the family-run business. An ESOP can ensure that the owner gets his or her money out and that the business survives. The advantage in selling to employees is that the owners are selling to people who have a vested interest in continuing the business. It also means that the owners do not have to show their financial information to outsiders who often are competitors. Change can usually take place with a tax-advantageous transfer and at minimal cost. Neither brokerage fees nor complicated legal costs have to be incurred to sell to employees. The major disadvantage is that employees may not have the cash to purchase the company. However, there are now many venture capitalists and sources of investment money that allow employees to complete a buyout. (Please see Chapter 4: Financing for ESOPs.)

> A print shop that was family-owned for four decades was up for sale in 1994. In the face of a potential sale and plant closure, the management group suggested an ESOP and buyout. Profits have doubled every year since the ESOP was set up, and 90 per cent of eligible employees participate as shareholders.

ESOPs AND BUSINESS FINANCING

ESOPs can provide a low-cost source of financing for business expansion. They can also assist in securing outside financing. For example, in the United States venture capitalists require an ESOP to be in place before investing in small or medium-sized businesses.

ESOPs AND RETIREMENT PLANNING

A number of economic indicators suggest that we are headed towards a retirement crisis in Canada. The OECD says the cost of our retirement benefits will triple between now and 2040. According to the Canadian Institute of Actuaries, only 14 per cent of the benefits that Canadians expect to receive after retirement will come from private-sector investments. The other 86 per cent will be paid from the taxes of future generations. Other independent surveys support that figure. An Ernst and Young/Angus Reid poll done in 1996 showed, nevertheless, that 43 per cent of taxpayers eligible to make an RRSP contribution did not do so. A survey by Marketing Solutions, a Canadian-based consulting company, shows that almost 70 per cent of Canadians have saved or invested less than $50,000, but economists estimate that Canadians need $800,000 in savings to sustain a reasonable lifestyle in retirement. Where will the money come from?

The US government recognized 25 years ago that ESOPs would give a broader base of citizens the opportunity to invest in their own futures and accumulate capital. Canada could do the same by changing tax laws and capital-gain provisions to encourage companies to implement ESOPs and employees to buy them.

The growth in the United States economy, its wealth accumulation, its lower tax base, its lower unemployment rate, and its lower interest rate, set it apart from the Canadian economy. One area that will start to diverge in the future will be the difference between what United States citizens and Canadian citizens will be have to retire on. The implications are enormous as our society ages and needs more funds to take care of its population. ESOPs give Canadians the ability to take care of themselves in the future rather than relying on governments to do this.

SPREADING THE WEALTH

ESOPs enable a greater cross-section of individuals to build personal wealth, to be recognized for their effort, and to share in the rewards. A broad-based ESOP is an investment in human dignity in that it recognizes and values the contributions of all employees. ESOPs encourage more broad-based stock ownership by giving the opportunity to participate in equity ownership to people who otherwise would not have the means to do so. As such, ESOPs can be an effective lever to share wealth and ownership. This is no small point when you consider that the wage gap has become a chasm, with a 300 per cent differential between the top 10 per cent and the bottom 10 per cent of income earners in Canada. Some people can afford to purchase shares in a company, but even a small investment, given the tax advantages and the growth of the capital value over years, would help each individual towards increasing his or her wealth.

Many owners believe that they owe a large part of their success to the hard work of their employees over the years and want to acknowledge this fact through a program of employee ownership. Employees also believe that the success of the owner had been through their hard efforts over the years. An ESOP is neither a paternal gift nor a right. It is in fact a great challenge that the owner is offering the employee—a challenge to take on a share of responsibility for the company's success and thereby enjoy the benefits of the rewards. With this inevitably comes the possibility of loss. It is critical that the owner not promise blue-sky results but be honest about the risks and rewards and treat the employee-owner with respect. Having said this, there is no question that the rewards generally far exceed the risks. In many cases employees have been able to leave companies with tremendous built-up wealth.

Before getting into the nuts and bolts of how to design and implement an effective ESOP program, let's examine what makes a good candidate for an ESOP program. The process itself is the key to a successful design and implementation. I will now outline that process and how it is central to the design issues that we will be discussing in Chapter 3.

CHECKLIST FOR ESOP CANDIDATES

Experience shows that there are key attributes that suggest a company is a good candidate for an ESOP. Review the following checklist:

- The ownership group is willing to share information and to share ownership.

- The company is in a fairly good financial position and is not in a turnaround situation looking for the employees to bail it out.

- The company has a history of maintaining its profitability and is likely to continue to grow.

- There's a specific need to share the responsibilities with the employees. This need may be to attract and maintain key people, a succession plan for the ownership group, or maybe there's a need to increase productivity within the company.

- For a broad-based plan there should be at least 20 employees in the company; otherwise the ESOP could prove an expensive task for the company to take on, due to the minimum costs involved for legal and accounting fees. For a key-person plan no minimum exists.

- The ESOP may be an opportunity for the company to differentiate itself from competitors. The ESOP may also be a competitive necessity if in fact the company's competitors have ESOPs in place.

- Where there's been a history of employee mistrust of management, as long as that mistrust is not too deep seated, an ESOP may be able to resolve the problem. Once an ESOP is explained to the employee group and has been put in place with the right intentions, any prior low morale or mistrust will generally dissipate.

- The amount of percentage of ownership that will be transferred to the employees will be defined in the process by the ownership group. It is not necessary to transfer 100 per cent ownership to the employees unless of course a succession plan is being contemplated. The percentage of the transfer is less important than the employees being able to participate in the potential growth of the company.

- Management or the owners must be able to listen to the employees. During the ESOP process management needs to take criticisms seriously and use them in the process to come up with a better plan. If management cannot listen to constructive criticism, the company may not be a good candidate for an ESOP

- The employees as a group must be interested in this type of scenario of equity compensation and be willing to listen to the presentation of an ESOP.

If the company is a candidate for an ESOP-type plan, whether it be equity, options, or phantom, the next step is to develop a process, which is key to implementing a successful ESOP.

THE ESOP TRANSFORMATION PROCESS: AN OVERVIEW

The process overview is illustrated in the flowchart below.

ESOP Transformation Process©

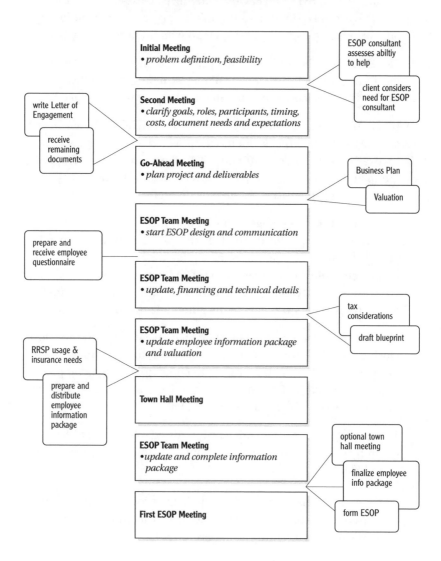

In some respects setting up an ESOP is much like taking a company public—in fact, you could call the process "taking it private" since the investment is available only to the employee group. The process starts with a feasibility plan, discussing problem, definition and clarification of goals. It requires outside consultants to do a due diligence review and establish a business value. The technical details—legal structure, tax considerations, financing, and type of equity—are compiled in a prospectus-like document, the employee information package, for the employee-investor. This all happens in a compressed time frame leading up to investment and the equity issue. Generally, the consultants utilized in this process include the business valuator the valuation of the company. Chartered Business Valuators (CBV) have special training in valuing private and public companies. Their organization is the Canadian Institute of Chartered Business Valuators, which is based in Toronto with chapters across the country. Other professionals of course will include income tax specialists such as Chartered Accountants (CAs) or Certified General Accountants (CGAs), and lawyers who are experienced in commercial and corporate work. At the end of the book there is a list of companies and organizations that can direct you to find the appropriate professionals.

The successful ESOP process first establishes the company's goals in implementing an ESOP and then juggles parallel tasks to design and implement and tailor the plan. It is an intensive exercise carried out over at least 14-weeks and requires total commitment from the ESOP team, consisting of the employer or owner, employee representatives, and consultants. Experienced project managers and open communication are key to success.

ESOP CRITICAL PATH

Process	Week
Goals and Strategy	1
ESOP Team Meetings	2–14
Education Seminar	3–4
Valuation	3–4
Legal Structure	3–4
Tax Strategy	3–4
Financing	3–4
Stock Plan	3–4
Draft Blueprint	3–4
Questionnaire	5
Feedback Loop	6–7
Employee Information Package	8–9
Final Employee Info Package	10–11
Town Hall Meeting	12–13
Subscription Meeting	12–13
Closing of the ESOP Transaction	14
Implementation	14+

The design process starts with clarification of the goals and method for implementing the ESOP and hiring of outside consultants who will do the work on the technical details of the plan—the ESOP structure, business valuation, shareholders' agreement, tax strategy, and financing. After that initial meeting, the ESOP team is assembled, a critical path agreed upon, and responsibilities allocated.

There are formal and informal communication channels built into the process. Employee representatives on the ESOP team bring issues to the table and provide ongoing feedback to their co-workers. Midway through the process the employee group is polled through a formal questionnaire. (A sample questionnaire is included in Appendix 3.) There are education sessions and distribution of an employee information package (a sample employee information package is included in the appendix as well). Once the ESOP closes, and the equity and/or options are issued to the new employee-owners, the implementation of the plan sets a new process in action—ongoing participative management. This post-ESOP program is discussed in Chapters 9 and 10 of the book.

ESOP GOALS AND STRATEGIES

The starting point for an ESOP is a fact-finding, facilitating exercise on the part of the ESOP consultant. A consultant, unlike the business owner, can give an independent third party view of the issues. It is also important to have the process under control. In many cases the owners have been promising some type of ESOP plan to their employees for as long as five years and have never done anything about it. The key to creating a successful ESOP is declaring the ESOP and then putting it into place efficiently and quickly. Business owners are very busy, and the ESOP may fall by the wayside. Through a process of interviews and corporate document research, the consultant will identify the goals and issues that drive the desire to put an ESOP in place. In most cases the ESOP is initiated by the business owner, but an employee group may also initiate it. The latter happens most often in cases of a leveraged buyout or a business rescue. Although ESOPs are usually the result of a practical purpose, there are philosophical implications that should be considered. An ESOP transforms a corporate culture, creating new lines of communication between management and employees. It creates a group of shareholders with a vested interest in the company's plans and decisions. In order to be successful, the plan design and implementation must have an ownership team with a full understanding of all the implications and total commitment from the outset. Experience shows that lukewarm or non-existent commitment will generally lead to a failed ESOP.

Therefore, in order to make the plan work, the commitment for success must include the allocation of key people and time to the ESOP project over a short time frame. That means the owners must invest their own time in seeing their project through. Key employees must also invest their productive time and work closely with external advisors. There also needs to be a general commitment to open communication and timely feedback.

Commitment Means Success

The success of an ESOP is a mixture of tangible and intangible ingredients, with common, underlying factors.

- It is a priority to all those involved.

- Employer and employees trust each other.

- Employee input is welcome.

- Immediate action creates results.

- Open and timely communication is achieved.

The Go-Ahead Meeting

Once the strategic goals have been clarified verbally and in writing, the ESOP consultant meets with the ownership group to determine the broad parameters of the ESOP, agree on the composition and design and implementation team, and commit to a critical path.

In terms of planning parameters, there are a number of key discussion points, which will be examined in greater detail later on in the book. For now, we will outline the process and all the things owners need to consider:

- Type of equity—basic tools are stock equity, stock options, or phantom stock units.

- Percentage of ownership to be offered—the ESOP can range from 1 to 100 per cent employee ownership.

- Sources of shares—from treasury (i.e., from shares that the company owns but they are not owned by the shareholders) or ownership group (i.e., shares that are owned by current owners and can be sold directly to the employees). If shares are purchased from treasury the proceeds of the investment go back into the company's bank accounts.

- Employee eligibility—there is generally a requirement for a continuous period of employment before a person becomes eligible for ownership.

- Allocation formula—the number of shares available to an individual will typically be a percentage of total shares available, based on an individual's base salary over the aggregate of total salaries. Allocation formulas can be based on different methods, salary being the primary method. Other methods could include merit, seniority, or attainment of target levels.

- Vesting period—where stock options are used, the plan will specify the length of time before they may be exercised.

- Buyout provisions—the shareholders' agreement will specify buyout provisions based on termination of employment, retirement, death, or disability.

- Share acquisition—equity may be sold or given to the employee free, but the ESOP is usually more successful when employees purchase shares. Employees take the investment much more seriously when they have to sign a cheque than when they are given something for free. The ownership group may then choose to match share-purchase with gifted options.

- Financing—equity may be purchases outright, granted in lieu of bonuses or acquired through a payroll deduction.

The consultant will outline the pros and cons of all options and work with the ownership group to determine which alternative best suits the company.

At the Go-Ahead Meeting

At the go-ahead meeting the scope of the project will dictate the composition of the team. Generally, the optimum is to have a wide range of input from the ownership group, external advisors, and the employees themselves. The ESOP is a process, and the greater the input at the beginning, the better results at the end.

Ownership and Employee Representatives

The ownership side should be represented by at least one or two of the owners, at least initially. The owners can opt to be less involved as the process continues. There should be one or two employee reps, depending on the number of divisions and the number of employees in the company. A good ratio of reps to total employees is one rep for every 100 employees. The employee reps may be picked by the ownership group or by the employees themselves, again depending on the culture of the company. It is very important to get a good chemistry on the ESOP team so that the plan proceeds smoothly and successfully with an efficient use of time for both the company and the outside consultants.

The employee reps are generally not brought into the loop until after the go-ahead meeting, when the issues have been finalized and the general blueprint has been drawn up.

Consultants

Finding the right consultants can be a difficult task. The first consultant to be chosen is the ESOP design consultant. He or she will be general contractors for the plan and it is his or her ability to choose the right sub-contractors that will move the plan efficiently forward. It is very important for the legal counsel to have expertise in corporate and commercial work, specifically in the areas of shareholders' agreements, share restructuring, and the ability to propose and help write the employee information document. Consider using the lawyer chosen by the ESOP consultant working with the ownership group rather than the lawyers who act for the company for various reasons:

1. These lawyers tend to be advocates of the owner's position and do not take the employee's position into account.

2. The lawyers may be specialists in certain areas but likely do not have ESOP expertise or commercial or corporate expertise.

3. The lawyers may not have the ability or motivation to ensure the assignment is done on time.

Tax consultants, can be chosen either by the ownership group based on people they work with or by the ESOP consultants. The business valuator can again be chosen by the ownership group or by the ESOP consultant in conjunction with the needs and desires of the ownership group.

TIME TO COMPLETE

The ESOP process generally takes three to six months, with the norm about 14 weeks. This time is needed to get the various parties to the table, to have an understanding, to present the education sessions for the employees, and to have everybody, including the outside consultants, the employees, and the ownership group, on side and agreeing to the elements of the plan. By the time the process is finished, a majority of the people buy in, having had input to the process.

Timetable

It is imperative that a formal timetable be drawn up and agreed to, starting with the closing date for the ESOP and working backward.

PRELIMINARY CRITICAL PATH

Date	Deliverable	Assigned to
January 28	Documents sent to Consultant	Company
February 7	Employee questionnaire developed	Consultant
February 23	Educational seminar presented	Consultant
March 1	Draft blueprint for review	Consultant
Mach 31	Final blueprint for distribution	Consultant/ Lawyer
April 14	Employee Information Package (legal document,forms, agreements)	Lawyer
April 26 to 28	Close ESOP transaction	Consultant/ Company/ Lawyer

This preliminary critical path would be filled out to include team meetings, finalization of caluations, financing, tax analysis, and town hall meetings (see page 18 ESOP Critical Path).

THE ESOP TEAM

The makeup of the ESOP team will depend on the size and scope of the proposed offering, and the company must decide and agree upon participants and their roles before the project can move forward. The core team includes the business owner, employee representatives, and external advisors. The external consultants will include the ESOP project manager, lawyer, accountant, tax accountant, business valuator, and potentially an insurance agent. Each member has a specific role in the process.

A word here about management. Key management generally may be one of the employee reps if the business owners are the key senior executives. In many cases however, the employee representatives are chosen from among employees.

Title	Responsibilities
Owner	Sets baseline parameters; represents company position and interests
Employee Representatives (1-3 reps generally)	Voices employee ideas, concerns, issues; reports back to employee group
ESOP Project Manager (generally outside consultant)	Determines feasibility, monitors timetable and budget, facilitates plan design and implementation, troubleshoots based on experience; implements organizational improvement and change; drives communication; oversees ongoing plan maintenance
Lawyer	Assures compliance to legislation, prepares shareholder's agreement; acts as trustee, oversees any necessary adjustments to corporate structure, provides basis for employee information package
Accountant	Assists with plan, inputs data
Tax Accountant	Prepares tax structure for ESOP, identifies tax effects for owners and employees
Business Valuator	Independently values company to determine share price
Insurance Agent	Responsible for funding of buy-sell employee insurance (this can be a necessity or optional depending on the needs of the company)

Other Consultants

Depending on the scope of the ESOP, there may also be venture capitalists or other financial representation on the team.

The team meets at regularly scheduled times to ensure the integrity of the communication process. Generally, the first couple of weeks will require more frequent meetings—perhaps two or three—then weekly meetings after that.

PLAN DESIGN

The core activity at this stage is the preparation of a draft blueprint based on the broad parameters agreed to at the go-ahead meeting. The ESOP consultant prepares a summary of all previous discussions and includes specific action that needs to be taken in formulating the plan. The blueprint also outlines all technical and financial considerations concerning the ESOP. There are three parallel activities in tandem with the preparation of the draft blueprint: the business valuation, the preparation of a tax plan, and legal structuring.

Business valuation is fundamental to the structuring of an ESOP in order to put a price on the shares, especially for privately held companies. This requires an independent appraisal to establish a fair market value (FMV), a valuation akin to the due diligence required when a company goes public. The valuator reviews the company's financial records, including past performance and future projections. He or she also reviews operations, interviews key managers, professional advisors, and customers, and researches the trends in the company's industry and marketplace economy.

Also important is feedback from the lawyer and tax accountant to ensure that the plan will meet all legal and tax legislation requirements. In order to structure the ESOP in a tax-effective manner, a review of the corporate tax structure and the personal tax positions of the ownership group is necessary. There are also tax implications relating to the financing and acquisition of equity by the employee group. The tax accountant does the reviews and prepares a tax strategy for discussion as part of the ESOP blueprint. The lawyer on the team is responsible for reviewing the corporate structure to determine whether any changes are necessary to comply with legislation. He or she also prepares a template agreement to cover the buying and selling of shares. This template is simply an outline of the initial shareholder's agreement. In-depth dis-cussions of these complex topics follow later in Chapter 5: Business Val-uations and ESOP, Chapter 6: ESOPs and Income Tax, and Chapter 7: ESOP Legal Requirements.

The ownership group and external consultants then meet to review the draft blueprint. This is a blueprint that outlines all the issues rele-vant to the plan for the employees. There is enough information at this point to completely appreciate the full scope and implication of the ESOP. The review stage is a natural turning point where the client may decide to stop the process. If the ESOP moves forward, the draft is revised based on discussions and then used as a new template for the creation of the formal agreements.

Communications and Feedback Loop

The draft blueprint is a structural framework of the technical aspects of the ESOP. Once it is accepted, the creative design work begins to address the unique needs of the company's culture. This is where com-munications are critical.

ESOPs are organic in that they mould to the company's nature. Input and feedback has to come from the employee base in order to create a true partnership and to engender trust in the process. In order to be successful with the design and implementation of an ESOP, open, two-way communications must be a priority throughout the design process—a continuous circulation and feedback loop.

The primary function of the ESOP team at this juncture is to for-malize the communication process with key objectives to circulate information and solicit feedback. A typical information flow would include the following:

- ESOP team includes employee representatives to consider draft blueprint.

- ESOP team drafts and circulates employee questionnaire.

- ESOP team reviews questionnaire results.

- Employee reps relay information between ESOP team and employees.

- ESOP team circulates employee information package.

- ESOP consultant holds employee education/information sessions.

- ESOP team hosts open forum for discussion of all aspects of plan.

- ESOP team accesses employee feedback, revises plan accordingly.

- ESOP team prepares final information for the employee information package, including legal documents, and hosts the town hall meeting and the subscription distribution.

Documents

The main documents of the communication plan are the employee questionnaire and the employee information package. The purpose of the questionnaire is to gauge employee interest in share ownership. In addition to ownership aspirations, it also serves to measure the level of knowledge about investments and ESOPs. The employee feedback guides the ESOP team in the technical design of the plan. The feedback also highlights the extent and the need for education sessions around investment. (The readers should review the typical questionnaire found in the appendices for further information.)

Education sessions would normally address how to read financial statements and include discussion of financial planning, tax planning, and the importance of independent legal advice. Other topics could be ESOPs, stock option valuations, etc. The employee information package and the ESOP package is much like that of a public offering, however, it is briefer and much less expensive to prepare. The employee information package includes a profile of the company, its history and its potential. The package also includes the company's financial picture and a summary of the valuation report that gives an idea of the company's worth and is used to help establish a fair market value (FMV) for company shares. The employee information package includes the blueprint as well as the legal documentation.

The culmination of the communication process is a town hall meeting where employees and their spouses can ask questions of the ESOP team in an open forum. Typically, the team outlines the design process, explains the choice of specific plan parameters, and discusses feedback from employees and its inclusion in the plan. The ESOP team assesses and considers employee feedback from the town hall meeting and makes final modifications to the plan. The team then prepares a final package that goes to the employees prior to the closing of the ESOP.

Although the process is driven by the executive team, it is in fact an outline that will be molded and shaped by communication with the employee group so much so that by the end of the process every stakeholder in the ESOP plan will understand the plan and support that plan as it is implemented.

The continuous flow of information between the ESOP team and employees, coupled with the will on the part of the company to welcome input and listen to employee concerns, helps ensure a high subscription rate and a successful ESOP implementation.

TRANSITION TO AN ESOP CULTURE

Once the ESOP transaction stage has been successfully completed, and the original goals of the owners and the employees have been met, the cultural transformation begins. The initial euphoria occasioned by the process has now given way to a time of getting back to work. The goal for the ESOP team during this stage should be to install a participative culture where employees start to act and think like owners.

Employees may now want to start acting like owners but they may be hesitant and uncertain about how to go about this. It is up to the board of directors to channel this new entrepreneurial energy and focus it on the goals of the corporation. At this point, a company must address four areas in the interaction with its employees: ownership, participation, training, and information. These areas will be discussed in more depth under post-ESOP issues in Chapters 9 and 10. To have a successful outcome for the ESOP, it is critical that the process outlined in this chapter be followed.

CONCLUSION

The next chapter will discuss some of the key design issues that will arise during the ESOP process.

Designing ESOPs

 T HE PROCESS OUTLINED in the preceding chapter is essential for arriving at the appropriate ESOP for a company. Design issues are of course critical to the foundation of the ESOP and whether it will be able to grow to meet the needs of the company in the future. Design issues must be reviewed in terms of each company's individual objectives and may have to change depending on the needs of the employee group.

WHERE DO THE SHARES COME FROM?

There are two sources of shares. Shares may come from treasury, which means the proceeds go back into the company's coffers, or they may come from the existing ownership group, in which case the proceeds go to the original shareholder. The deciding factor on sources of shares is influenced by the purpose of the ESOP. If the shareholders are looking at the ESOP as a means of liquidating one of their major assets, they will probably decide to sell shares to the employees. That way the owner receives the cash from the employee, the employee receives the shares, and the owner has his or her liquidity. The other alternative, if the owner is seeking not liquidity but working capital for the company, then he or she would issue shares out of treasury. The shares then would be issued from the company out of treasury to the employees, and the money from the employees would go back into the company's bank account.

For example, if an employee bought 1,000 shares at $1.00 a share, the owner would receive $1,000 and the employee would receive $1,000 worth of shares. For our example we'll assume the company had $10,000 shares owned by the owner at the start of the transaction. After the sale to the employee, the owner would have 9,000 shares, and the employee would have 1,000 shares. If, however, the owner issues treasury stock to the employee, the employee would pay $1,000 to the company and receive 1,000 shares. The $1,000 paid by the employee would stay with the company. The company now, however, would have 11,000 shares. They would be made up of the 10,000 shares previously owned by the owner and 1,000 new shares that were issued by the company. Therefore, in this transaction, the owner would have 10,000 of 11,000 shares, and the employee would own 1,000 of 11,000 shares. If the owner wished to allow the employee to own 10 percent as in the first example, the company would restructure and issue 20,000 shares to the owner for his previously 10,000 shares, and then allow the employee to purchase 2,000 shares from the company, thereby owning 2,000 of the 20,000 or 10 percent of the company.

Shares from Treasury

Treasury shares are those that have been allocated through the company's corporate structure but have not yet been issued. Companies that want to use stock options as a means of attracting and retaining staff tend to issue shares from treasury. They do so because the liquidity issue is not a major concern for the ownership group. Liquidity is an issue only when the ownership group wants to take money out of the company. The amount of money raised through ESOPs is not usually significant when the main aim of ESOPs is to attract and retain people. At other times, raising money from the employee share purchase is the main aim of implementing the ESOP. An owner may liquidate a portion of his or her own shareholding with the express purpose of raising capital or for the acquisition of additional assets to help the company grow.

From a corporate confidence perspective, it is powerful to be able to demonstrate to employees that the proceeds from the shares they purchase are staying in the company to help expand and grow the company. Another way to look at this is when an employee is being asked to sign a cheque to actually give money over for acquiring those shares, if the employee realizes that the money is staying in the company and being used to expand the company he is much more confident in his investment. In contrast if he believes that the owner is just taking the money out of the company and leaving the employee with the risk of expanding the company he may feel less willing to participate. It is important to understand that there is a major difference for ESOPs that are introduced in a public versus a private company he may feel less willing to participate. In a public company if the employees want to purchase shares they can do so through a stock exchange. In a private company, the only shares available are those of the current owners or through the treasury of the private company. Decisions regarding what shares to issue differ tremendously, depending upon whether the company you are investing in is public or private. Public companies tend to always issue out of treasury shares and therefore create a dilution when they are looking for additional equity. Private companies, on the other hand, have the option to issue out of treasury or the owners can sell their own shares.

Shares from Owners

In cases where an owner's major assets are tied up in the company, an ESOP may be implemented as a means of freeing up some capital for the owner's personal use. Owners do that by selling their personally held company shares. When employees buy ownership shares, they buy directly from the actual shareholder. This often gives rise to questions about why the ownership group is selling equity or giving any kind of option plan in a company. It is important for the ownership group to allay any concerns employees may have and to recognize that there is nothing wrong or unusual about recouping net worth in the form of proceeds from shares. Eventually the employees themselves will want to liquidate their assets for the very same reasons as the current ownership group.

Combination of Shares

An ESOP implemented as a succession or exit strategy must satisfy the owner's financial need in leaving the business and the business's need for ongoing financial health. In such cases, the source of shares may be a combination of ownership and treasury.

Dilution

Any time shares are issued from treasury, the current shareholders' percentage ownership is diluted. For example, assume there are two shareholders, each owning 50 percent of a company. There are 10,000 common shares authorized in the company, of which 1,000 have been issued to the two owners. If a further 9,000 treasury shares are issued to employees, the two current shareholders move from a position of owning 500 shares each in the company that had 1,000 shares issued, or 50 percent of the company, to owning 500 shares in a company that has 10,000 shares issued, which effectively reduces them to 5 percent ownership of the company. That's an extreme example, but it is important that the ownership group as well as the employees understands dilution. Although the owner's percentage has decreased, the actual value has not because the 9,000 shares that have been issued out of treasury have raised the value of the company because the money raised by selling those shares has gone into the company and therefore increased its value. There's been no change in the value of the owner's shares, only of their percentage.

NUMBER OF SHARES

The structuring of the share issue often highlights the fact that the actual number of available shares is inadequate. More than 80 percent of the time the corporate share structure cannot support an ESOP. I have seen some private companies that have only three shares issued. Obviously to issue shares to another 100 or 200 people, more than 3 shares will be needed. It then becomes necessary to increase the number of authorized shares, not only for immediate ESOP needs but also to support future growth. Increasing the authorization of shares is not a difficult issue. A corporate lawyer will amend the company's articles of incorporation to increase the number of shares. In some situations, perception may dictate volume of stock. Employees may prefer to get 100,000 shares each valued at 10 or 20 cents a share rather than 100 shares worth $20 each. The decision on how many shares each employee receives is dependent upon the sophistication of the employee group and the feedback received from the employee questionnaires.

STOCK SPLITS

If there is insufficient stock to issue as a company grows, the stock may have to be split. This entails additional legal and accounting fees and a communications effort in terms of explaining the intricacies of a stock split to the shareholders' group. For example, if an employee owns 500 shares of a company and the stock splits 2 for 1, after the stocks split the employee will own 1000 shares of the company but the value of those 1000 shares will remain the same.

CORPORATE STRUCTURE

When discussing the source of shares, additional consideration should be paid to the current ownership's tax position. The tax advantages for owners of a Canadian-controlled private corporation (CCPC) will also come into play as a retiring owner will want to take advantage of the $500,000 capital gains exemption currently available to owners of a CCPC.

This may lead to a restructuring of some of the ownership position, so as to maximize his or her tax position. For example, an owner may decide to capitalize on the capital gains exemption to set up a separate holding company and/or an offshore company. The new structure should be discussed and evaluated for the impact it would have on the company going forward.

EMPLOYEE ELIGIBILITY

There is usually an employment requirement for a person to be eligible to participate in an ESOP. This can range from immediate eligibility to up to two years of continuous employment, and it will vary depending upon the nature of the company, its culture, and its training cycle. For example, if it will take two years to assess whether an employee will be a real contributor to the company's growth, a lengthy eligibility period is appropriate. Typically, established manufacturing companies require a longer qualifying term. The reason for this is that there is a longer learning curve in manufacturing facilities for both knowledge-based and technical employees. In the high tech or knowledge-based field where there is a high demand for talented employees, the eligibility norm seems to be between three and six months. Even within a plan, there needs to be room for flexibility, allowing for variances for key people. For example, if a company requires a senior sales person to start with the company immediately, and wants to issue stock options to that employee, the plan will allow the company to waive the eligibility requirements so that key person could be hired.

Generally, a company wants enough time to determine if an employee fits into the corporate culture. A probationary period also saves the company administrative headaches by avoiding having to collapse ESOPs for employees who are not working out in the corporation.

The eligibility factor highlights the fact that the issuance of stock, stock options, or phantom stock is not a right of the employee; it is a benefit that the company confers on those employees who have put effort into growing the company. The eligibility requirement, however short, establishes that share ownership is not given out to just anyone, but that employees must earn the right to become a partner in the future viability of the company.

ALLOCATION FORMULA

The number of shares allocated to an individual employee will generally be a percentage of total shares available, based on the individual's base salary as a percentage of total salaries. However, there are other ways of allocating stock or stock options. Base salary may be coupled with seniority, level of management within the corporation, or departmental targets. An allocation formula is important for several reasons. It tends to create a level playing field because perceived fairness is important for employees. An allocation formula makes the plan administratively convenient for a company as it can allow new employees to be incorporated into the plan fairly easily. It also allows the employees to do a quick calculation of what they are entitled to, which again reinforces the concept of fairness.

For the majority of companies, the individual's base salary is the most common method of allocation. The culture of the company will define what works best for each kind of employee. For example, if there exists a cadre of people who have been with the company for a number of years, and whose salary would not be a fair representation of the contribution that these employees have made, some seniority component must be put into the allocation formula to account for this.

Generally, an allocation formula is the same for all people in the corporation; however, differentiations between different positions or levels within the company is possible by adding or subtracting from the formula. Everyone is treated equally in the sense that the formula is calculated fairly for each person in any particular position. The best way to determine an allocation formula is in the initial meetings with the ESOP team when the particular issues (i.e. cultural) of the company can be discussed and the various formula applications put forward. It is only at this point that you have input from the owners, the advisors, and eventually from the employees themselves, from which you can arrive at an allocation formula that is fair for everybody.

VESTING

Vesting gives employees the right to exercise stock options and become equity shareholders. Exercise price is usually set at or below the fair market value (FMV) on the date the option is granted. The employee is guaranteed that price for a fixed period of time until a specified future date when share options vest in title to that employee. Vesting means that that person has earned a right to be able to exercise the option and buy the shares. Normally, vesting is based on a time element whereby the employee earns the vesting after having been employed for a certain length of time. For example, a four-year vesting period with 25 percent vesting each year means that for every year that the employee is with the company, he or she earns the right to purchase 25 percent of the total number of his or her allocated share options. Other means of earning options can be tied into performance so that when certain targets are achieved by an employee or by the company, stock options become vested with the employee. For example, the stock option plan may state that if the company increases its revenues by 30 percent the employee's stock can be vested at that point. The employee's stock does not get vested until the company has grown revenue by 30 percent. Performance options are valuable to companies because they do not dilute the company until such time as the company has grown in certain revenue or profitability targets that has some application to wealth creation and therefore some minimization of the dilution factor. Vesting usually takes place at the beginning or end of the year. With vesting the employee receives all the stock options immediately and can exercise them at any time because there is no waiting period involved. This is used fairly selectively, usually to attract senior people to a company. Most companies will have a vesting period ranging from three to five years with the percentage allocation spread over that time frame. The term of the stock option is usually between five to 10 years. This means that employees have that period of time to exercise their right to purchase the shares at the grant price. If the options are not exercised within that time, the employee loses the option to purchase the shares. There are many tax implications for both private and public companies to the granting of stock options. These are discussed in full in Chapter 6: ESOPs and Income Tax.

BUYOUT PROVISIONS

In a private company the only way the employees will be able to turn their shares into cash is if there are agreed-upon terms in the shareholders' agreement. An ESOP is basically a long-term plan, a method for employees to generate wealth and benefits due to the increase in the wealth of the company. In a public company there are generally fewer problems with liquidity because employees can sell shares on the public market at any time. However, in a private company this is not the case, which is why shareholders of private companies can sell only when a third party purchases a company or when it goes public with an IPO. Given changing circumstances and the volatility of life, not all employees will be around for this liquidity event. One of the key philosophies in an ESOP is that there should be protection for the employees who are continuing to be employed by the company, balanced with fairness to the people who are leaving for various reasons. An ESOP should avoid a situation where many leave, take value with them, and leave the employees who are staying to pick up the pieces.

There will be cases of death or disability, bankruptcy, separation, or divorce, all of which may effect employee shareholdings. There are also retirement circumstances or the case of an employee being fired. Generally for the sake of fairness, employees who are no longer employed due to death, disability, or retirement will receive fair market value for their shares. The question is how to deal with employees who leave for any other reason. Most companies pay a discount anywhere from 25 to 75 percent of the fair market value and spread the payments over a certain number of months. The board of directors always has the authority to overrule the buy-sell provision in special cases. For example, assume an employee is fired within two years of joining the company. This employee has contributed to the company, but because he or she is leaving before the company has fully realized its growth potential it is unfair to give the full fair market value for the employee's shares. This employee may receive 50 percent of fair market value rather than the 100 percent received by an employee who stays for a five or 10 year period.

The buyout can be a difficult issue for both owners and employees who have different perspectives. Although leaving, employees may feel entitled to full fair market value for their contribution to the value growth of the company.

For employee owners who are staying, the value that the departing employees have contributed may not be realized through an equity event for many years. Employees may question whether it is fair for people who are leaving to receive fair market value when there is in fact no liquidity to those shares. To balance these opposing issues, companies generally pay less than fair market value when people leave for reasons other than death, disability, or retirement.

Understandably, employees want to know how they will be able to sell their shares in the future. The shareholders' agreement covers this. There is usually a "tag-along" clause that ensures that if the existing majority shareholders agree to sell their shares in the company, the employer-owners have the right to tag along or to sell their shares at the same price. There may also be a "drag-along" clause that states that if the majority shareholders agree to sell their shares in the company, they have the right to drag along the employees or require them to sell their shares at the same price.

The company may also create a mini-market where employees can sell their shares to other employees, usually once a year. This helps create liquidity for shareholders who are leaving or who want to cash in some of their gains. The mini-market may be supported by the company or may be strictly an arrangement between employees. Many employers will put a mini-market clause in their shareholders' agreement if they're in the type of company that's not likely to be sold or go public within five years. Because of this, the mini-market generally does not start before a five-year time frame, and in some cases even longer than that. The result is that employees will have to be with the company for a period of five to 10 years to see some liquidity in their shareholdings.

However, if an employee does leave before this five-year period, then the shareholders' agreement applies, and the company is required to buy back those shares at either fair market value or a discount. This is called a repurchase liability. This means that the company is building up a potential liability because when people do leave, the company has to buy back those shares. How that buy back is funded and what impact it has on the growth of the company is important.

Generally a company will purchase key person-insurance to fund the buyout provisions of the agreement for key employees such as senior-level executives. For the stock in general, a company would tend to consider some type of modified sinking fund that would be put aside at the end of the year for people who are leaving. A sinking fund is a fund or a reserve into which funds are deposited and available to buy back shares. The key element in any buyout provision is that both the employee group and the ownership group understand that this is a contractual arrangement in which the employees are agreeing to invest in the company, and the company is agreeing to make sure that the growth value will be reflected in some type of liquidity to the employees at some point in the future. The amount to be set aside in a sinking fund is determined by the individual company, and it depends upon their cash flows, future projections of profitability, and what the company needs for short-term and long-term expansion strategies. Without any liquidity provisions in the shareholders' agreement the stock is, in effect, of no value to the employees. This, of course, defeats the whole purpose of the ESOP, the creation of a participative environment, and sharing in the wealth of the company as it grows.

As you can see, clear communication between the employee group and the ownership group and an understanding of the shareholders' agreement and liquidity provisions are critical. However, the ownership group must be very careful to ensure that they are not restricted in decisions about a third-party offer or IPO. The legal agreement must be structured in such a way that the employee group must go along with the original ownership group's decision as to what is necessary for the company. An ESOP does not reduce the fiduciary responsibilities of the board of directors or of the ownership group to increase the value of the company for all employees. For example, if the original ownership group wants to sell portions of their company in the future, the employees generally will have the right to sell the same percentage as the ownership so that they are not disadvantaged. Such legal provisions ensure that the ownership group is not being restricted as to the long-range viability and strategy implementation of the company.

The commitment of the ownership group is key to the success of an ESOP and therefore the ownership group has to feel that if it decides the company should be sold in the future, it cannot be restricted from making that decision. However, the proceeds from that sale will be distributed equitably among all employees, depending on their percentage of ownership.

SHARE ACQUISITIONS

Equity may be sold or given to the employees, but an ESOP is more successful when employees are required to purchase a certain portion of shares. The ownership group may then choose to match share purchase with gifts. In the United States studies of high-performance companies over the last 25 years have shown that there are four elements for their performance: participation, training, ownership, and information. The element that we are talking about here is the ownership element.

There are many plans that comprise only stock options. Certainly, stock options do have the ability to motivate and retain people. Stock options may allow employees to participate in the wealth that they've created. However, in terms of long-range growth and retention and attraction of people, stock options themselves are limited because there is no downside risk to the employee. They do not invest any money in the company. If the company goes up in value, employees make money, and if the company goes down in value, they don't lose money. The employees do not assume a risk position in a company. They do not take that investment as seriously as they would if they had invested money in that company.

True ownership of a company occurs when a cheque has been passed from the employee to the company and the employee owns legal title to those shares. For example, once an employee is actually an owner, participation, information, and training become more real and are approached with more passion. A good analogy is a person who owns a house versus one who rents one. The mindset of the owner is completely different from that of the tenant or even the rental property owner. The same of course holds true in the ownership of shares in the company; the level of commitment is much higher in the ownership of an asset. The actual number of shares that are held is not as important as the fact that the person actually does own those shares in a company.

PORTION OF OWNERSHIP

The ESOP can range from 1 to 100 percent employee ownership. The percentage that's offered is not as critical as the fact that shares or options are being offered at all. Generally, initial ownership offers of between 10 to 20 percent of the value of the company are sufficient to create the benefits of an ESOP, within a company. As can be imagined, in a privately owned company, the current ownership group does not want to dilute its ownership position more than it has to. Many owners have struggled and sacrificed for many years to build successful companies. This must be discussed thoroughly with the ownership group so all owners fully understand what's at stake in allowing an ownership percentage to be sold or given through stock options to the employees. Generally, there are opposing forces in this area. The ownership group as a rule wants to give up less and less, and the employees want more and more. If the percentage of shares offered is too low, less than 10 per cent, the employees will regard the offer as being not a true intention by the ownership group to share the rewards of the company. On the other hand, unless the ESOP is being put into place for succession planning, or if too much of a percentage is given out to the employees initially, it becomes more difficult for the owners to keep control of the company and to implement their strategies going forward with the company.

As a general rule of thumb, no matter which percentage is chosen, employee groups will likely pressure owners to increase the percentage as time goes by.

Employees, on the other hand, are coming into a company that has passed its initial risk stage and is into the secondary and tertiary levels of risk. The highest risk for any company is in its first five years of ownership. This is because the company has not established a history with its customers or suppliers and hasn't created conditions of stability that tend to reduce risk. As a company survives longer, its risk reduces somewhat as it moves into different phases. It has the ability to weather recessions, and has clients and suppliers who have helped it grow while still maintaining a viable operation. Often employees do not appreciate the amount of effort and sacrifice that the original ownership group had to make to get the company to this stage. As such, it seems that no matter what percentage of the company is offered to employees, it is perceived by them as not enough. So a key element of any ESOP plan is to manage expectations and to make sure that the employees understand the reasons for the percentage offered. Most owners tend to pick this number based on what other companies and similar industries are doing, hence the 10 to 20 percent figure.

FINANCING

Stocks may be purchased outright, granted in lieu of bonuses, or acquired through payroll deduction. The investment is like any other for employees, and ultimately, the onus is on the individual to research, question, and analyze whether it is beneficial to them. The individual must be comfortable with the investment of his or hers hard-earned money in this company. An ESOP investment is just that, a business investment. The major difference, of course, is that the employee has some control over the future growth of the particular ESOP investment.

Generally speaking, when financing ESOPs:

- The company may loan funds to employees so that they may invest in the company.

- The employee may use funds from an RRSP or borrow money from the bank and utilize a current RRSP to fund this investment (subject to Canada Customs and Revenue Agency restrictions as outlined in Chapter 6: ESOPs and Income Tax).

- The employee may borrow money from friends, relatives, or the bank to invest in the company.

- The company may allow the employee to purchase the shares through a payroll-deduction plan.

- If the company has a bonus plan that has been set up in concert with the ESOP, future bonuses may be used to acquire shares in the company (see the use of bonuses in setting up plans in Chapter 6: ESOPs and Income Tax).

- There are a number of tax implications depending on the type of financing used which are discussed in the section on taxes in Chapter 6: ESOPs and Income Tax.

ADMINISTRATION

The administration of an ESOP is an area that is not well addressed but is very important to the ongoing success of the ESOP plan. There are two methods for dealing with the administration issues: internal and external. A company may choose an internal person to do the administration tasks regarding new hires and employees who leave. Alternatively, a company may hire an outside, third-party trustee to do the record-keeping and keep the company informed of changes in legislation that may affect their plan. Administration issues are discussed more fully in Part Two of the book dealing with post-ESOP issues. The company must decide whether it has the internal capability for handling the administration or must look to an external source. The items that will help the ESOP team decide on this issue are as follows:

- What is the annual turnover rate of the company?

- Is there an HR person already onboard or will one be hired?

- Are the company's benefit plans taken care of internally or externally?

- How does the company communicate and administrate its current benefit plans?

- Is the current administration of employee benefits and resources satisfactory, or will an external person be needed in the future?

- Does the company like controlling its administration issues, or does it have a history of sourcing them out to third parties?

- What is the cost of using an internal person versus the cost of an external party?

The administrator, whether internal or external to the company, is the "face" as far as employees are concerned. The employees will be content with a plan that is administered in a way that provides them with timely, relevant information when they need it. The administrator must respond promptly to all employees' requests and be able to interpret the plan rules. Should employees be unhappy with the administrator, their perception of the plan as a benefit to them may be tarnished.

For example, poor record-keeping of employees' allocations can result in misunderstandings and in increased tension between management and employees. This is true especially if the plan has increased in value over time.

A key decision by the ESOP team is to decide whether or not to appoint an internal administrator or go to an external advisor. The advantages of an internal administrator are:

- face known to employees,

- part of the corporate culture,

- faster response time to employee concerns,

- knowledge of the plan, and

- may be a participant in the plan.

The disadvantages are:

- costly,

- ties up valuable HR time that can be used in other areas, and

- learning curve

The advantages to hiring an outside administrator are:

- cost containment,

- no learning curve,

- specialized administrative advice, and

- outsourcing of HR needs.

The disadvantages are:

- unknown to employees,

- response time may be slow, and

- not involved in company, therefore, distant from employee concerns.

Whether an inside or outside administrator is chosen, his or her tasks will be as follows:

- is main contact with employees,

- deals with questions about the plan,

- handles all document approvals,

- deals with reporting and tax obligations, and

- advises employees when options are exercised or when shares are redeemed.

Choosing Administrators Using an RFP

It is always best to obtain several quotes if deciding to use an outside administrator. A Request For Proposal (RFP) to be sent to prospective trustees, custodian, and administrative service providers would include:

- A description of the ESOP plan.

- An outline of the company history and future.

- A request for the following information about the administrator company:

  - Their corporate history and experience in providing stock plan administration, including how much of their business resources are devoted to these services;

  - A clear description of their system for plan administration in terms of logistics, accuracy, efficiency, flexibility, timelines, and problem resolution;

  - Information on the range of investment availability such as whether they can facilitate cashless transactions, diversification, real time trading, and private stock transfers;

- A transition plan.

- Steps they take to educate employees on issues relating to their current stock plan, employee ownership in general, financial planning, taxes, and retirement planning.

- A clear outline of all costs associated with the plan for both the company and the employee, including the billing schedules and out-of-pocket costs.

- References to be contacted during the evaluation process.

- An evaluation of the proposal, which would include both cost factors and intangible factors:

  - A cultural fit. The service provider should understand the company's business and be prepared to deal with employees as the company itself would deal with them.

  - A clear long-term commitment to the business. The provider must have the financial muscle to remain in the stock option administration business.

  - A highly trained staff experienced in stock option administration. The right service provider will have invested substantially in the training and development of its employees.

  - State-of-the-art technology. The right outsourcing firm will have superior technology to provide complete administrative services, and the right service provider will have a flexible and extensive technology platform.

  - A formal transition process. The right service provider will be able to offer a clearly defined process to transfer records from the company provider, and minimize the company's involvement in the transition process.

  - Well established quality controls. The provider will have a system of checks and balances in place to ensure quality throughout the administration of the company's stock option plan.

  - A process for assessing client and employee satisfaction. The right vendor knows the importance of company and participant satisfaction.

COMMUNICATION

Initial Announcement

The initial announcement to the employees is a key milestone in the plan. This signals to the employees that the company is serious in proceeding with the design and implementation of an ESOP. Many companies have been talking about implementing an ESOP for years. The hiring of an ESOP consultant as well as meeting the proposed timetable will create a sense of excitement and urgency among the employees. It is important to maintain this excitement through a serious of communication pieces.

Follow-Up Communication

The next major communication piece is the Employee Questionnaire (See Appendix 3). The purpose of the questionnaire assesses the level of interest of the employees in the plan and determines the employees' motivation to join such a plan. In addition, employees' knowledge in this area can be assessed. The results of the questionnaire allow the ESOP team to focus on key issues. For example, how much education will have to be offered to the employees for them to have an understanding of the plan? What is the employees' preferred means of financing the plan? Employee representatives on the ESOP team maintain ongoing communication with the employees. This can be on an informal basis or through a formal meeting whereby employee representatives brief the employees on the status of the plan.

Communication Document

The initial stage of the ESOP process produces a blueprint that clearly outlines the proposed plan. The blueprint contains information on all the technical issues concerning design of the plan: is it a share purchase, stock option, or phantom plan? The relevant legal and accounting issues are also addressed. The blueprint is created by the ESOP team and written by the ESOP design consultant.

Once the blueprint is accepted as final by the ESOP team, it is given to the lawyer to draft into "legalese." At the same time, it will become the basis of the employee information package, which will be provided to all participants.

Education Seminars

An education seminar is generally provided to the employees concerning the technical aspects of an ESOP in the areas of accounting, law, tax, and valuations. This seminar is usually produced by the ESOP consultant in conjunction with one or more members of the ESOP team. Usually the owner or an employee representative is involved. At this session, the details of the company ESOP are not discussed however the general issues concerning in ESOPs and their impact on employees are explained.

Town Hall Meeting

The final stage of communication is the Town Hall Meeting, which is attended by all participants and the ESOP team. It is held as a means to explain the Employee Information Package and to answer any questions from the employees. At this stage, the ESOP is about 90 percent complete. Based on the results of the meeting, the final plan is prepared, and the employees usually have one to two weeks to decide whether or not to participate. Sometimes, however, the Town Hall Meeting will be the end of the process, and the employees will take home the final Information Package at that point.

COMMUNICATION ISSUES FOR MULTI-SITE, MULTI-TARGET AUDIENCES

The communication phase for multi-site, multi-target audiences includes two stages:

Stage I—Communication Planning

- Create and finalize communication objectives and project timing.

- After communication topics have been discussed, the team should develop specific objectives with respect to the two targeted groups: the employees and the presenters. The management group might also be targeted separately. Finally, a detailed time line for all aspects of the project should be drawn up.

- Prepare a roster of the involved presenters. This roster would include the presenters' names, locations, job responsibilities, presentation experience, and immediate support staff. This step is necessary to plan the implementation of the project as discussed in Stage II.

- Keep an inventory of all corporate benefit communication pieces and production materials.

- Collect available generic ESOP materials. Generic cost-effective ESOP materials are available from the National Center for Employee Ownership. These materials may be integrated into the company's communication program.

Stage II—Implementation

Implementation planning includes the following:

- Communication Content: The basis of any communication program should, of course, reflect and enhance the objectives of the plan. The content of the communications program will include three general categories: what the plan means, what the plan comprises, and how the plan fits into the company's culture.

  - What the Plan Means: This includes a discussion of the philosophy of the plan, why the company adopted the plan, and what it means for the future.

  - What the Plan Is: This would include an explanation of how the plan operates and how it benefits participants.

  - How the Plan Fits into the Corporate Culture : This would address the impact on the day-to-day operations of the company and the fitting of the plan with the company's business strategy.

- Targeted Audiences: If there are several distinct audiences to whom these objectives will be communicated, the appropriate objectives for each audience should be emphasized in all communication pieces.

- Communication Materials: The first communication piece is a comprehensive written document that forms the basis for all communication materials, which are then directed to the appropriate audiences. The company reviews and approves these pieces prior to the production of any other communication materials.

As part of this work, the ESOP consultant will inventory all corporate benefit communication pieces and production materials. This inventory will help determine what information has already been provided and to what extent there should be compatibility of graphic layout and narrative style. In addition, it may be possible to utilize existing artwork in the production process to achieve cost savings.

- Communication Components
  - Slide presentation which would include detailed speaker's notes that each of the presenters would use at each of their respective locations.
  - Question and Answer booklet, which would anticipate questions that the attendees might ask and which could be referred to after the meetings.
  - ESOP brochure, which meets the communication objectives mentioned above.

Upon completion of the communication materials, meetings for eligible participants would be held in the company's offices. To facilitate these meetings, the ESOP team will:

- Conduct a meeting with the presenters to review delivery of the ESOP communication program at their respective locations. The meeting will address presenters'questions regarding the ESOP plan, specific program content, and communication techniques in general.

- Develop an implementation strategy for each location. The strategy will include the number and location of employee meetings and focus on any differences in corporate culture.

- Assist in presentations as required to provide feedback and suggestions to the presenters.

- General Considerations

The design, implementation, communication, and administration of a broad-based ESOP is a complicated effort involving a number of individuals both inside and outside the company sponsoring the plan. To facilitate the ESOP process, designate one primary contact at the company for the operational aspects of this engagement. That person will liase with the ESOP consultant, presenters, and outside advisors. (The company's legal counsel should review and approve all materials for conformity with applicable provincial, and federal laws.)

THE ESOP TEAM

Having the right team will influence the success of the ESOP process. Chapter 2 discussed how the team is chosen and the importance of the team's chemistry. Ownership commitment is also critical; ESOPs initiated by the ownership group, in terms of a buyout have the highest chances of going forward and being successful. However, ESOPs initiated by a lower level of management, the HR group, or from employees, without a strong commitment from management, have a fairly low success rate. Of course control rests with the ownership group, and that group must be convinced that the process will succeed. Therefore, for an ESOP to succeed, the ownership group must have a vested interest in seeing the process go through. Management will follow the ownership group's lead. It is just as important to manage the expectations of the management group as all the other employees within the company.

Owner Members of the Team

The owner, or the owner's representative on the team, will usually set the parameters for the ESOP as well as represent the company's position and interest. This person must have 100 percent commitment to the employees becoming partners in the company. Obviously, the owner or executive must be a person respected by the employee group, or the process will fail. This trust and respect may not even be there at the beginning, but certainly by the end of the process after having worked as a team the important element of trust will have been built and used successfully in negotiating and in launching the ESOP.

Owners who have the traditional mindset of the hierarchy of ownership -pyramid levels- will find it difficult to implement an ESOP. The hierarchical way of running a company has proven successful— but not with an ESOP. When employees are asked to invest their money, without any change in responsibilities or interest, trust and respect do not result, meaning an inconclusive or a non-satisfactory ESOP. On the other hand, an owner who passes information to employees, shares profits with them, and involves them in decision-making, will find it easier to create an ESOP.

Employee Representatives

The owners are one part of the project team. Next are the employee representatives. These people give voice to the employees' ideas and concerns and report to the employee group as a whole. The employee reps are important to the success of the project. They may be chosen by the owners or elected by the employees themselves in a democratic vote. The method chosen really depends upon the culture of the company. The majority of companies that implement ESOPs tend to have the owners pick the employee reps because the ownership group is more likely to pick a person with the ability to discuss issues both with the ownership group and with the employees to the benefit of both groups. The employee rep must have a good rapport not only with the employees but also with the owners.

In organizations where direct representation from the employee group is required, such as in unionized workplaces, electing the reps is valid. However, if there are three employee reps, at least two of them are likely chosen by the owners. The employee reps are very important to the chemistry of the process. They must have good conceptual abilities, wide experience within the company, and communication skills to report to their peer group. Most importantly, they must have the trust of their peer group. Nonetheless, it is critical not to bring the employee rep into the ESOP process too early. Owners must set their parameters without the influence of employees. That's not to say these parameters won't change over time, and in fact they do, but the owners must be able to speak freely regarding their concerns. For example, such issues as percentages to be transferred, vesting requirements, and the allocation formula, are all critical issues that have to be openly discussed between the ownership group and the ESOP advisor before they are put forward as a position. Employee reps are brought on board after the initial stage of the blueprint has been completed. The owners explain the blueprint to the employee reps, who go back and explain it to the employee groups; therein is created the constant feedback loop. This is key to the success of the process. Employee reps bring enthusiasm and issues that are important to the employee group, as well as some tremendous ideas. The ESOP team is always improved by this constant interaction between the employee reps, employees, and the other members of the ESOP team.

External Members of the Team

The pivotal player is the ESOP consultant or project manager. The project manager can be either an internal or an external person. However, I believe an external manager is more suited to making sure that the assignment is done on budget and on time and, more importantly, that all stakeholders feel they can talk to an unbiased external person. The project manager facilitates the initial meetings and decides whether or not an ESOP makes sense for the company and whether one can be implemented. The project manager also monitors the timetable and the budget, to bring the assignment in under budget and on time. Every ESOP runs into some obstacles which can be overcome by an experienced ESOP project manager who troubleshoots and gets the project back on track.

For example, many times the ESOP project manager has to coordinate a meeting among members of the ESOP team and, without constant calls and focusing on what is important, those meetings fail to take place. Or documents have been provided for all parties to review but because of workplace pressures, these documents are never reviewed. The ESOP project manager not only reviews these documents to make sure that they meet the needs of the ESOP but also ensures that everyone has reviewed them and understands them.

An ESOP project manager also implements organizational improvement and change that is used to help drive the ESOP communications. For example, the communication models that are used within the corporation prior to the ESOP may have to be changed to meet the needs of the ESOP. One company implemented intra-web broadcasting so that it could provide the educational seminars and the town hall meetings with its employees across the country. This worked so well that the company is now utilizing this methodology for training programs.

ESOP project managers also provide ongoing plan maintenance such as communicating changes in the nature or conditions of the plan. For example, a stock split or the need to introduce a new share or new option program will require additional communication materials, which the project manager is really in the best position to provide.

In Canada, ESOP project managers are available from

- Large accounting firms such as Deloitte and Touche and PricewaterhouseCoopers.

- Large human resource firms and compensation firms such as William Mercer and Towers Perrin.

- Smaller specialty boutiques.

The ideal consultant is the one who best meets the company's needs. Those needs change depending on size, industry, and project. Some project managers specialize in large public companies, while others concentrate on smaller private companies. The criteria for choosing the ESOP project manager is similar to choosing any other consultant, one where chemistry and the philosophical approaches to the implementation of the ESOP are critical. When choosing consultants the following questions should be posed:

- What is your philosophy towards ESOPs, and how do you implement an ESOP?

- How many ESOPs have you implemented over the last three years?

- What's the nature of the companies that have utilized the ESOPs you've developed? What is their size and geographical location?

- How do you budget the project? Do you have a fixed fee or do you charge a fee plus?

- What other services do you offer such as taxation consulting, business valuations, legal services?

- Can you provide three company references?

- What problems can we expect in implementing an ESOP, both pre-ESOP and post-ESOP issues?

- What makes your firm unique?

There is a wide variance, even among project managers with similar experience, with regards to fees, so it is important to obtain at least two or three quotes. The Chart below discusses potential fee ranges.

Specialty	Fee ($000) Over 1000 employees	Fee ($000) Under 1000 employees
ESOP Project Manager	50–250	5–50
Business Valuator (for private companies)	25–50	5–15
Taxation Specialist	25–50	5–12
Lawyer	100–200	10–25

Lawyers

Lawyers are a key component of the ESOP team. A lawyer will ensure compliance as well as prepare the various agreements such as the shareholders' agreement, the ESOP agreement, and any trust agreements that may be necessary. Any good commercial or corporate lawyer will be able to provide this service. In addition, the lawyer oversees any necessary adjustments to the corporate structure. It is important to choose a corporate lawyer, commercial lawyer, or a tax lawyer because he or she has the technical skills to help implement ESOP plans effectively from a legal standpoint. Nevertheless, it is important to remember that lawyers are advocates who advocate a client's position. This is fine in an adversarial legal situation. But in an ESOP situation the goal is to avoid an adversarial position, and it is essential to have a balanced approach from all ESOP team members. This means that the lawyer must treat all stakeholders equally, including owners, managers, and other employees.

Not all lawyers understand the importance of ESOPs or are willing to learn this process. The owner's lawyers tend to advocate a position for the ownership group, which is what they are paid to do. However, this can cause major problems in terms of delaying the ESOP and creating animosity among the various stakeholders.

The lawyer must agree with the ESOP philosophy. A naysayer will inhibit the process. Before selecting a lawyer, the owner should ask for his or her opinion of ESOPs. The response is usually very clear. To reduce legal costs it is important to bring lawyers in towards the middle or end of the process, after the blueprint has been prepared by the ESOP team. At this point the lawyer can review the blueprint for legal concerns and it can then be discussed with the employee reps.

Accountants

The accountant will assist with the formulation of the business plan, to calculate impact of the ESOP on the company's bottom line, and help formulate the financial statements to be presented to the new investors. The company accountant is usually best suited for this role. However, the tax accountants required may be either internal to the company or external. The tax accountant must be knowledgeable in the areas of preparing tax structures for ESOPs and have the ability to iden-tify the tax effects for both the owners and the employees. Because tax is such a specialized area, outside tax advisors are generally used. As with a lawyer, the tax accountant must believe in ESOPs. Any reluctance on his or her part can cause delays and create animosity. ESOP consul-tants can provide names of tax accountants who may be suitable for the ESOP team.

Business Valuators

The value of any public company is established by the public market-place; not so in a private company. That is why a business valuator is necessary to independently value the company to determine the share price, or to determine the stock option price. Ownership groups often resist having an independent valuation done for ESOP purposes, due to the cost involved. However, an independent valuation accomplishes several things. First, no matter how much the employees trust the own-ership, when they are asked to invest in the company, it is better to have the value of the company established by someone who does not have a vested interest in it. Second, there is also a fiduciary responsibility to come up with a fair value, and the ownership group may not be in the best position to provide an unbiased viewpoint. The value put forward by a third party is viewed as having more credibility than one done internally. Third, the owners also must realize this valuation may be used for other purposes. For example, if there is a shareholders' dispute after the ESOP is completed, the valuation may be used as support. Fourth, an independent valuator can help the company set up a formula to value itself each year or the valuator can come in and update his or her valuation to keep it current.

Insurance Agents

Last, but not least, is the insurance agent. In roughly one-third of ESOP cases, an insurance agent is needed to oversee the buy-sell agreements for the key employees. The reason especially for small- to medium-size companies that rely on several key people to grow the value of the company, the risk is a loss of one of those key people. However, this loss can be insured against through the buy-sell agreements. The insurance provides funds to help continue the company in case one of the owners or senior people die or are disabled. This insurance is an important part of keeping the company's value if there's a catastrophe involving any of the key people. The insurance ensures the company continues as well as provides the key person's estate with an insurance payout. The buy-sell agreement is in effect funded by key-person insurance.

TROUBLESHOOTING

A number of problems may come up during the ESOP process. Knowing what these issues are and being prepared for them will help minimize the impact on the plan. These issues will vary among companies, but others may appear during the process as well.

Financial Health

If the company is not earning enough money or if it does not have a large enough asset base, asking the employees to put money into the company is seen as little more than bailing it out. An ESOP can be successful in a turnaround situation. In fact, studies in the United States have shown that ESOPs help in nine out of 10 turnarounds. However, it is unfair to ask employees to be involved in a situation where the ownership group is not willing to continue to fund the operation because of the risks associated with the company. A turnaround is a very special situation and should not be undertaken lightly. It should involve turnaround specialists who can assess the likelihood of achieving some kind of growth and value for the company. Turnarounds are outside the scope of this book.

Expectations

One has to manage expectations not only among the employees but also among the ownership group and the management. When an ESOP is announced many people, especially if they are in the high-tech environment, think they are going to become instant millionaires. This just isn't the case. There is a risk to investing in any company, and that risk is not diminished by implementing an ESOP. This risk has to be explained and communicated very clearly to all the parties involved. Unless some unusual equity event such as a third-party acquisition, or a liquidity event such as an IPO, takes place, people should not be looking at an ESOP as a generator of instant retirement funds. The type of expectations will differ of course depending upon who the stakeholder is. The owners will expect instant gratification and total gratitude from the employees for having sold them shares. This will not happen; employees will be glad to be part of a company but will not show much gratitude towards the owners for doing something that they feel they deserved in the first place.

Management will also believe that the employees should be grateful for this opportunity and that the owners should be glad that the management is willing to buy into the company. Management also will believe that it deserves the majority of the shares being put forward and will in all likelihood feel that whatever amount of shares it received is not enough. Employees' expectations will be of instant wealth as well as instant respectability. All these issues are dealt with during the ESOP process through communication and feedback.

Clearly Defined Goals

When the ESOP process is underway, there may be times when there are major disagreements between the groups involved. For example, the ownership could disagree with the employees or the management could differ with ownership on the question of the number of shares that are being allocated to each of the groups. The resolution of any disagreement has a great impact on the success of the plan. Issues are raised because they are important, and they need to be worked out in an appropriate way. This is where the blueprint with the ownership group's clearly defined goals and commitments comes into play. The blueprint can be used to benchmark and set a limit on what is feasible and what is not, which will help solve many of the disagreements that may arise. In effect, the process itself is a dispute-resolution mechanism and allows for disputes to be identified, clarified, and solved by the ESOP team.

Team Chemistry

Although team chemistry has been covered earlier in this chapter, it is a point that bears repeating. The chemistry of the various team members is critical to the success of the ESOP. The team needs people who want to develop a solution that is fair and equitable for everybody involved. With the right team the process flows smoothly, and the results are sound. On the other hand, when there are people obstructing and favouring one particular group over another, problems will result. There's always the risk that either the ESOP will not succeed, or if it does that there will be hard feelings on all sides. Team chemistry is one issue that's not to be taken lightly.

Time

The ESOP process needs enough time. It is neither practical nor reasonable to cut the process short. A proper job will take three to six months. As long as people realize that something is being done, and is being done fairly and professionally, they are prepared to give the ownership group the benefit of the doubt. Mistrust arises when owners try unsuccessfully to meet unrealistic deadlines. If a promise is made in an ESOP process it must be done within the timeline.

Disclosure

Nothing will kill an ESOP faster than the discovery of a statement that is untrue. For example, if the owner truly wants to liquidate some of his or her shareholdings because his or her major assets are tied up in the equity of the company, that should be stated to the employees. Although the owner does not have to indicate what those funds will be used for, he or she must indicate that the purpose of the ESOP is to transfer those assets into cash. Employees must be made to understand that there is nothing wrong with that. When employees are asked to become partners and investors in a company they expect and deserve full disclosure.

Realism

An ESOP is not a magic bullet; it is an investment with risk attached and needs to be acknowledged as such by all parties involved. Companies can't afford to make promises they can't keep. For example, a strategy such as an IPO should not be guaranteed by the management group; there are no guarantees. Rather, an IPO could be put forward as a long-term goal. Realism comes into play because employees want to know how they are going to liquidate their investment so that they can realize the wealth that they may create over the years. It is critical to define the exit strategy for the company, whether there's a third-party sale, whether it is an IPO, or even how long the employees will have to wait for that liquidity event.

Experience

Employees may have past experiences with plans that did not go well, but far from being discouraging these experiences can offer valuable insight to avoid the pitfalls of the past.

Through the employee questionnaire, the ESOP project manager will elicit the experiences of employees in these areas and see what areas can be improved upon for the current ESOP plan.

Participation

Not everyone will buy into the plan. Some people will not take any financial risk. Expect this. An ESOP does not need all employees to buy in, but it would be surprising if more than 20 percent of employees did not buy into a company that offered a well-thought-out ESOP plan.

Studies have shown that participation levels in private companies generally are much higher than those in public companies. Public company take-ups usually are in the range of 20 to 40 percent while a properly implemented private company ESOP will range between 70 to 90 percent.

Culture

Studies have shown that a participative culture is crucial to the ongoing success of an ESOP plan. Once the ESOP plan is in place the company needs to be run with employee participation. Management may require training to develop a more participative style. (See Chapter 8: Administration and Communication.)

Administration

Companies must be practical in administrating the plan. Whether a company chooses an internal or external adminitrator, the key to a successful plan is always the KIS Principle, "Keep It Simple."

Communication

In most cases, employees want more shares than are available to be sold or to be given out. The management group should explain how the number of available shares was calculated and why these shares are being given up. Communication can forestall erroneous perceptions. For example, if employees believe that the plan is too small and has no significance to them, the motivation for retention and attraction that may have been one of the key features of putting a plan into place may be derailed.

Most ESOPs in Canada and the United States will have an ESOP of 10 or 20 percent of the outstanding shares either through equity or stock options. A company that gives out less than 10 to 20 percent is running the risk of being perceived as stingy and not being fair to employees.

CONCLUSION

This chapter has reviewed the objectives of the ESOP. Readers know how to determine whether a company is a potential candidate, started the process of designing the ESOP, and looked at the communication and troubleshooting issues that will arise during its implementation. These issues, although critical to the success of an ESOP, are basically non-technical issues, in the sense that they do not involve meeting certain legal and accounting requirements. The next few chapters will go into detail of the practical requirements for the plan and how these impact the design issues that have already been discussed in the previous chapters. Chapter 4 looks at financing, and how it affects the decisions that have been taken for ESOP planning in the blueprint.

Financing ESOPs

THERE ARE TWO ASPECTS to financing an ESOP. Each depends upon the purpose of the ESOP. This chapter deals with employee financing, in other words, how and where does the employee obtain the funds to purchase equity? Then corporate financing is discussed; where does the company look to obtain corporate financing in partnership with the employees if required, for example, in a succession plan or in a management buy-out situation.

EMPLOYEE FINANCING

Options for financing an ESOP are as numerous as the creative minds that conceive them. What underlies them all is the need to instill a sense of ownership and commitment in the employees, ensuring that they make a financial commitment to establish the ESOP either through a cash investment or other financial obligation. Employees are undertaking an investment in the shares of a company that entails a real risk. This investment is similar to any other investment that they may make, and employees should be fully aware of the risk. Let us examine some of these methodologies in more detail.

Employee Self Finance

Employees who have sufficient financial strength may purchase shares in the company directly, using their own spare cash, loans from a financial institution or from family and friends, lines of credit from their banks, or their RRSP funds. In some cases the company itself will set up a method to loan funds to the employees so that they may purchase shares in the company. The shares are held in escrow until such time as the loan has been repaid. Another way that employees may self-finance is if the company allows them to use their bonuses to buy shares instead of taking cash. The tax implications of setting up such a plan are discussed in Chapter 6: ESOPs and Income Tax. Another way for employees to purchase shares is through payroll deductions. This can be done on an ongoing basis where the company deducts money to purchase the shares from the employee's paycheque. Typically in most share plans the methodology chosen by the employees is based upon the amount of the investment and whether or not this will cause an investment hardship for the employees. Many broad-based ESOPs do not require a significant investment by the employees for the ESOP to be successful. In most cases the investment by individual employees will be anywhere from $500 to maybe $5,000 as a norm. Also to be considered is the complexity created for the company in terms of administration. Obviously, a plan where employees can have a payroll deduction or use their bonuses to obtain the shares will be more complex than one where the employees can either pay by cash or by some loan arrangement with an institution or through friends.

In privately held companies a useful method to aid the employees in financing the company is called the Freezing technique. In effect, the founding owners freeze the value of the company at a certain date. The value is then converted into preferred shares which are owned by the founding shareholders. However, once the preferred shares are in place a new common stock can be issued which has a nominal value, as all the company value resides in the preferred shares. These common shares are then issued to the founding shareholders as well as the employees. In this way, the employees can own common shares in the company for a minimal cost. As the company grows in value, the increase is attributable to the common shares, not the preferred shares, the value of which remains fixed at the value on the "freeze date." Since this has many tax implications, the technique and appropriate capital structure should be done by professional tax experts.

The advantage of this employee financing is the ability to participate in growth at a minimal cost. The disadvantage is the tax and legal costs to freeze, and the difficulty of communicating the freeze technique to the employees.

Variations of this technique can be used. For example, it is possible to freeze only a portion of the current value, and thereby issue the common shares at a value greater than a nominal one.

Bank Loans and Company Guarantees

The company may make an arrangement with its bank so that participating employees can get bank loans to purchase shares. The shares serve as security for the loans and usually the company guarantees the loans to ensure the best interest rate and encourage the bank to participate. Because shares in a private company are not very liquid, they can serve as collateral security only when the major part of the guarantee is supported by the company. Companies tend to do this in situations where they have substantial dealings with the bank. This loan becomes part of their loan security agreement. To guarantee the loan the company must have a good relationship with its bank or lending institution, and the bank must have experience in loaning these amounts to a number of employees without creating an administrative nightmare for the company with the ESOP. Not all banks or lending institutions want to get into this type of arrangement. Therefore, it is important that the company first discuss this methodology with its bank before discussing it with the employees.

The advantages of this type of program are that the employees are required to obtain a loan and sign a cheque to the company, which serves to ensure that the employee is taking this investment as seriously as any other type of investment. The company must review its own balance sheet to make sure that it could guarantee such a loan and whether or not it was in a position to encourage this type of borrowing from its employees. As a general rule for privately held companies, management tends to encourage employees to buy shares with their own cash before borrowing through the company.

Company Finance

If the company is not using the ESOP to raise capital either for internal purposes or to purchase a portion of the shares, it may finance employee share purchases by means of a note receivable from employees. In this case the note receivable is held by the company, which is taking the place of the bank or the lending institution by loaning money to the employee to acquire the share capital. Employees then repay the company over a set period of time, say for example, five to 10 years. Interest may be charged on the note receivable, depending upon the needs and conditions of the company and the employees. Notes receivable may also be used with employee bonus programs, and the repayment terms may include a mandatory percentage of any future bonus awarded until the debt has been retired. For example, if the company loaned $2,000 to an employee for a period of five years, and the employee was able to obtain a bonus each year of $1,000 a year, that employee could use a percentage of the bonus, say 50 per cent or $500, to repay the loan, so that way the note receivable is retired, and the company does get equity into the hands of the employee.

If the company wishes to assist the employees to establish the ESOP, but the company does not have sufficient existing resources, external financing will be required. Loans to the company in this type of financing program are similar to those of the bank loans where the company is the guarantor of the loan. If the company is in a strong financial position and is capable of allowing this debt to be held by the company without upsetting its lending ratios, then the company may be in a position to offer this to employees. If the company has a financial position that is somewhat tenuous or, is in a very volatile industry where it may need its credit leverage to raise financing for internal working capital purposes, the company may not be able to risk loaning employees capital to purchase equity. Other issues that must be addressed are buy-back agreements with the employees that would deduct the amount of the loan still payable to the employer from the payroll check of an employee who is leaving.

For most companies implementing an ESOP, the most satisfactory method, with the least amount of risk to the corporation and also the lowest administrative cost, is to have employees provide funds to purchase the shares either through their own resources, lines of credit, RRSPs, or future bonuses.

Sources of Outside Capital

In situations where the employees are purchasing shares in the company for an equity buyout it is important to look at some type of partnership with an outside purchaser. Whether a management buyout or a broad-based plan, many employee groups do not have the funds to close the deal. An exception is if the employees are looking at a buyout planned over a number of years. Buyouts may be planned over five or 10 years to purchase the current ownership position without going to an outside party, but in many situations, even in a long-term buyout succession plan, some type of third-party investment will probably be necessary at some point.

When sourcing capital the availability of debt and/or equity capital will depend on the financial strength of the company, the industry in which it operates, and the philosophy of the current owners. The following are some of the principle capital sources that can provide the funding needed to partner ESOP with an employee buyout.

Commercial Lending Banks

As discussed above, a company's bank should be the first consideration for employees obtaining financial assistance in buying shares. When the company wishes to assist employees directly, but lacks the capability of doing so, the bank can provide assistance through loans or through lines of credit to the individuals. Banks tend to respond to a competitive approach and will be generally aggressive in vying for business that they view as attractive. Banks that have a good relationship with their clients will not want an outside bank to provide loans for an ESOP and therefore encroach upon that banking relationship to the company. This gives the necessary leverage to the company to go forward with this type of lending. In a partnership situation, the bank will also be able to look at loaning money on a leveraged basis against future assets of the company.

Asset-Based Lenders

For companies with significant assets in the form of real estate, equipment, or financial capital, asset lenders may provide an opportunity to achieve more flexible financing than can be obtained from commercial banks. An example of an asset-based lender would be the Business Development Bank of Canada (BDC), which will loan based on covenants on these assets. These convenants tend to be less onerous in repayment terms and are more tailored to the company's situation.

Sub-Debt Providers

The share equity divisions at the banks and certain specialized financing firms will provide capital that is often referred to as quasi-equity or mezzanine financing. Sub-debt is subordinate to the security interest held by the primary debt holder, which is usually the bank. Higher interest rates are applicable to this type of financing, reflecting the riskier position, and the company is required to issue some form of equity compensation as well, usually in the form of a warrant, which is issued as a nominal amount. A good source of this type of financing is, again, the Business Development Bank of Canada, formerly the Federal Business Development Bank (FBDB). A sub-debt provider creates for a company the ability to loan funds at a higher interest rate that is not solely based on assets but also on the future potential of the company to grow and earn income. Because these lenders will loan money based on future potential of a company, a higher interest rate is charged. Because the sub-debt lender will be in a secondary position to the primary lender, which may in this case be a bank. In return, the sub-debt lender will usually take back preferred stock in the company with the option to convert to common stock at some future event.

Institutional Equity Sources

These include mutual funds, pension funds, labour-sponsored funds, and insurance companies, as well as the capital divisions of banks and other lending institutions. The capital division of the bank loans money based on the company's future cash flows rather than its asset base position. Each institution has its own criteria for deals, which may include

- preferred or prohibited industries,

- stage of development,

- size of deal.

Generally these lenders are attracted to companies that tend to have excellent future prospects and good management. Institutional equity lenders generally want to be able to liquidate their investment within a short time frame, usually five years, and they look for an annual rate of return of at least 30 per cent. Although specific terms of the investment and the rates that an investor would enjoy are negotiable, it should be noted that these investors tend to protect their investment in several ways. They usually want board representation with the right to approve fundamental matters such as the annual budget, major changes in the strategic direction of the company, and solicitation of additional investment.

Venture Capitalists

Venture capitalists (VCs) are similar to institutional equity sources, however, they tend to want to invest more in earlier-stage companies and start-ups. Venture capitalists will also consider smaller investments, but they generally want a much greater level of involvement and a much higher rate of return on their investment.

Private Equity Sources

Wealthy individuals can be a source of capital. However, it is difficult to find these people, and according to their particular risk tolerance, they may or may not want to invest in a particular company. Access to these individuals is generally initiated by the company owners or through brokers or agents.

   If the purpose of the company's ESOP is to engage the employees in the participation of the future growth and wealth of the company, and the accumulation of the investment is not of particular importance to the company, the source of the capital will likely be from the employees themselves. However, if the purpose of the ESOP is to implement some type of succession plan for the current ownership group, or to raise new capital for the company for expansion, some type of partnership arrangement between the ESOP and outside corporate financing is more likely.

CONCLUSION

This chapter has outlined the methods employed to achieve financing for employees and for the corporation, depending on the ESOP's objectives. Once the financing is in place, the ESOP can move forward into the technical details. Chapter 5: Business Valuations and ESOPs, addresses a key technical step, the business valuation.

CHAPTER FIVE

Business Valuations
and ESOPs

T HE INFLUENCE OF A BUSINESS valuation on the successful implementation and continuation of an ESOP is immense. Whether the ESOP consists of an equity share, a stock option, or a phantom unit, the employees need to know the value of their ownership in the plan. When employees know the outcome of the valuation, the company may better use participation in the plan for purposes of measurement, motivation, and team-building. It is important that the employees are kept up-to-date on the value of these plans on a periodic basis. Keeping the employees fully informed creates trust between the employees and the original ownership group as it verifies in the employees' eyes that a partnership truly has been formed, creating a strong foundation for the company going forward.

Business valuations are both art and science. On the artistic side, business valuations involve business judgment and experience in a real-world setting. The scientific side involves the selection of appropriate valuation methodologies, analysis, and research, which apply to specific industries and the purpose of each valuation assignment. By properly balancing these elements, a business appraiser will be able to arrive at a successful and fair valuation.

VALUATION TERMS

Each profession, be it law, medicine, or astrophysics, relies on jargon to communicate specific concepts. In business valuation, it is important to understand the terms "fair market value," "fair value," and "fair price," as these are central to all ESOP valuation assignments.

Fair Market Value

The accepted Canadian definition of fair market value is "the highest price expressed in terms of money, or money's worth available in an open and unrestricted market between informed, prudent parties who are under no compulsion to transact and who are dealing at arms length."

"Highest price" is the maximum price the purchaser is willing to pay to acquire the shares and the minimum price alternatively that the vendor is willing to accept to sell those shares. Typically when there is a transaction these two price ranges will intersect. It is important that valuations always be viewed from both the purchaser's and the vendor's point of view. If there remains a significant difference outside of what is considered a normal valuation range, the valuator must be able to logically resolve this difference. Normal value range will generally be plus or minus 25 per cent.

The expression "money or money's worth" means that the transaction price is defined in terms of cash or cash equivalents. An example of a cash equivalent would be a note taken back payable at full interest rates and fully secured by collateral assets. It is important to understand that any terms that can be attached to a transaction can have as great an impact on value as the valuation itself. As an example, if a purchaser offers to purchase a company for $1 million, but the terms indicate that the $1 million will not have to be paid for 100 years at no interest, then clearly the purchaser is telling the vendor that the company has little or no value in terms of its current cash value.

Now consider "open and unrestricted market." Fair market value calculations are hypothetical and therefore occur in a notional market. They are not transactional in a sense that company A signs a cheque and cash is transferred into the bank account of the owners of company B. Because fair market value is notional it is assumed that all purchasers have been included in the marketplace. Whether or not there are specific special purchasers in the marketplace must be considered, and if identifiable special purchasers do exist, they must be taken into account in the valuation. Many types of companies have an active market for the sale of their assets or shares of their company. Examples of these types of companies would be cable television, radio stations, funeral homes, or school bus operators, and in this kind of situation special purchasers can be clearly identified through a formula methodology.

What is the meaning then of "informed, prudent parties"? Fair market value assumes that both the vendor and the buyer have equal knowledge of the financial affairs of the company. The concept assumes that the purchaser, being a rational investor, will base his or her final decision on the sound economic merits of the investment. In the practical world, economic decisions are but one factor in any transaction, and therefore it is critical that the final valuation number makes sound economic and business sense. As an example, a transaction may occur in a company where the ownership group is selling to its major supplier, who, having special knowledge of the industry, will look at the acquisition in terms of not only the economic impact but also the impact that the acquisition will have in terms of its market position, name branding, and relationship to other competitors.

In the world of fair market value the expression "no compulsion to transact" exists; no one is forced to buy or sell. However, for purposes of calculations this does not prevent the transaction from occurring as it is assumed that both parties will eventually arrive at the highest price in the marketplace. This assumption does tend to remove both the bargain-basement sale price and the premium purchase price due to non-economic pressures. Therefore, bargain-basement sales or premium purchases should not be used as comparables when assessing value.

Fair market value also assumes that all parties are dealing at arm's-length, that is, between parties who are not related and who have negotiated in good faith to arrive at a price. The reason for this inclusion is obvious since fair market value is done in many cases on non-arm's-length transactions, where parties are related by family or common ownership.

Fair Value

Fair value is a widely used term that, unfortunately, has never really been defined. The term is used in various provincial securities acts as well as the *Canada Business Corporations Act*. It has usually been interpreted by the courts to mean fairness to minority shareholders. In this context, no minority discount is generally applicable in a fair value calculation. A minority discount, which will be discussed later in the chapter, is a reduction in the purchase price to account for the lack of control by the minority shareholder. The fair value calculation can be used for ESOPs involved in public companies rather than private companies, since the former are always quoted on the exchange in minority stock values.

Fair Price

There are as many prices for a business or an asset as there are purchasers. However, in the notional market, there is only one fair market value. Real-world buyers or purchasers are able to pay bargain or premium prices due to synergies in the form of value-added profits they bring to the acquisition. For example, if there are four purchasers for one company, each of those purchasers will make a bid that has a different value attached to the shares. The reason for this difference is that each company will have a different economic and non-economic reason for purchasing those shares. One company may want to include this company in its worldwide holdings and believe that this acquisition will increase its public share value. Another company might be able to increase its gross margin by integrating the product line of the company it is acquiring. Another company might be buying out the competition and, therefore, be able to charge higher prices for its products. The fourth company may be buying the company to acquire its work force. So each company does its own calculation of value and will arrive at a different price. Each of these prices of course are relevant; the vendor will have to decide which of the deals based on the terms and conditions of each offer are in its best interest, both from an economic and non-economic viewpoint.

What is Fair Price?

The fair price *may* equal fair market value but only by coincidence. Open market transactions result in sales that can be influenced by illness, retirement, lack of motivation of the original ownership group, and in purchases driven by the need for expansion, the desire to manage, or to gain prestige from the acquisition itself.

As an example, many of the values attributable to the purchase of sports teams are driven not so much by the economics of the acquisition of the sports team but by the egos of the owners who want to own sports teams.

Any open market transaction between arm's-length parties is at a fair price, since a transaction is evidence that both parties have acted in their own interests. Open market values do not normally reflect fair market value; because of this, comparables can be very misleading, and their relevance in reaching valuation conclusions debatable.

The following diagram illustrates the relationship between a fair price and fair market value:

Bargain Purchase	Fair Mkt Value (Fair Value)	Special Purchaser A	Special Purchaser B	Special Purchasers C
$ $100,000	$500,000	$600,000	$750,000	$1,000,000

If one knew that a price paid was a bargain, for example $100,000, or was based on a special purchaser concept, for example $600,000, then one could infer fair market value as a sub-set of the price paid, say $500,000.

Fair Market Value Versus Fair Price

Fair market value or notional valuations are generally used for estate planning purposes and in dispositions upon death. They are not pricing exercises but pure fair market value assignments. No identified special purchasers are taken into account in the valuation process, which is performed to satisfy tax authorities. In the real world, however, every buyer is a special purchaser and tends to pay for an asset based upon particular needs. A real transaction is therefore a pricing exercise, not a fair market value assessment.

Fair market value exists only in the notional marketplace, not in the real world. For one thing, fair market values reflect the perfect world, which does not exist; for another, a buyer's perception of value differs for each individual or company.

In the notional world of fair market value

- Parties of equal negotiating and financial strength arrive at the highest price available.

- There are no restrictions on the sale.

- Concepts of forced or imprudent sales do not exist.

- Parties are aware of all relevant information.

- Transactions are always at arm's length.

- Transactions occur only on a cash basis or a cash-equivalent basis.

- Non-commercial goodwill is excluded from consideration.

- The market is unrestricted as to who the buyer will be.

In the real world of fair price

- Parties rarely have equal negotiating strength.

- Prices do not correspond to the highest price available.

- A company may be restricted to selling certain classes of shares.

- Sales can be forced, and imprudent sales are normal.

- Information is never fully known by both sides.

- Non-arm's-length transactions are common.

- An all-cash basis is not the norm.

- Non-commercial goodwill can be paid for.

- The number of buyers is limited due to competition and knowledge.

Fair market value is non-existent other than in the notional marketplace. In the real world, a purchaser may pay a premium above fair market value to achieve economies of scale. These economies include a reduction of the competition, acquisition of new management expertise, new customers, and new sources of supply. Therefore, each purchaser can calculate a unique price for the same asset, and this price is usually a different number than the fair market value. The vendor can only estimate at the savings that the purchaser may accrue and does not have access to the full scope of information necessary to arrive at this higher value. In any event most purchasers will tend not to pay for these synergies unless they are forced to through a competitive bidding situation. Alternatively, the vendor may be in a position of having the sale due to personal circumstances and the purchaser, knowing this, may buy at a discount from fair market value.

Fair Market Value and ESOPs

Business appraisers use fair market value rather than fair price when calculating the value of companies for ESOPs, because ESOPs are, to a certain extent, designed to meet certain tax criteria. The *Revenue and the Federal Income Tax Act* require for purposes of meeting its criteria that fair market value be utilized in any calculations of valuation between arm's-length or non-arm's-length parties. This requirement holds true for stock equity plans, for stock option plans, and for phantom unit plans. The goal of the act is to ensure that the employees are receiving a fair calculation of value. It may not be the value that the company could be sold for, or the value that the company will go public at, but it will be a value as based on methodologies that are fair and acceptable to the Canada Customs and Revenue Agency for purposes of implementing and designing the ESOP. Taxation issues will be discussed more fully in Chapter 6: ESOPs and Income Tax.

Minority Discount

The value of stock owned by minority shareholders is different than that owned by majority shareholders because a majority shareholder controls the use and disposition of the assets of the corporation. This control over one's investment makes a majority holding less risky and therefore more valuable.

This factor is at work daily in the public market. Publicly held shares are constantly traded on a minority-based price. However, when a takeover bid of the whole company is announced, the bid price can be as much as 40 per cent greater than the trading price. The reason for this premium is that the acquirer is obtaining a control position.

There is no specified discount percentage that can be applied to a minority shareholding in a closely held company for ESOP purposes. Each case has to be examined on its own merits. However, numerous studies in the United States have shown minority discounts generally start at 30 to 35 per cent of the *pro rata en bloc* value and are adjusted up or down from there depending upon circumstances. The *en bloc* value of a company is a calculation of the sale price of the company assuming 100 per cent of the shares of the company are sold. For example, a shareholder with a 10 per cent ownership in a company valued *en bloc* for $1 million may receive only $70,000 instead of $100,000, because a 30 per cent minority discount was applied to the *en bloc* value.

Minority values are important in the context of ESOPs because most ESOPs are implemented by transferring minority shares to employees. Although in total a significant amount of shares might be transferred, on an individual basis, the number of shares is usually rather small. Therefore, a minority discount should be applied whenever a fair market value calculation is being calculated for purposes of an ESOP, except where the minority shares in total make up a substantial portion of the outstanding shares. My experience has shown a normal discount rate applied in an ESOP calculation around 25 to 35 per cent. This lowered discount results from the fact that in most ESOPs there is a substantial buy-sell or shareholders' agreement in place that defines the liquidity of those shareholdings and allows the minority shareholder to realize some value at some point in time down the road. This tends to reduce what otherwise would be a higher minority discount that could be applied to those shares.

Contingent Tax Liability

In completing a valuation, it may be necessary to revalue fixed assets such as real estate, machinery, and equipment that have fair market values exceeding those recorded on the book of accounts. The theoretical or potential sale of these assets gives rise to contingent income tax liabilities. Examples of these contingencies would be capital gains, recaptured depreciation, or terminal losses. The valuator frequently has to assess the likelihood of payment of these taxes and account for them in some manner, in the valuation price.

For example, a company may own real estate that was purchased in 1965 for $500,000 and is worth $2.5 million in today's marketplace. If that property were sold today, the company would have to pay income tax on the capital gain net of any disposition costs, as well as tax on recaptured depreciation. However, since the company is a going concern, it may not sell this property for 10 to 20 years hence. The valuator must decide, based on the facts, what, if any, quantum of contingent taxes should be applied to the asset value of the company.

Goodwill

There are two general types of goodwill, commercial and personal. Commercial goodwill, by definition, can be conveyed to the buyer and, due to the conveyance, can be said to have value. Personal goodwill, on the other hand, is considered to be specific to a person and therefore, when that person departs, he or she takes the value of that goodwill with him or her.

For example, a world-renowned brain specialist in practice would be considered to have personal goodwill, since the particular skill that attracted the patients would leave with the specialist. However, an engineering company with a complement of support staff, work in progress, and a large clientele may have both personal and commercial goodwill. The latter would have some value.

The difficulty the valuator faces is separating the personal from the commercial goodwill component. This is done by assessing the likelihood of sustaining revenues, identifying the key persons in the organization, and investigating comparable transactions occurring both inside and outside the organization.

Synergistic Purchasers

A synergistic purchaser is a buyer that, due to special circumstance, will pay more for a business than is justified purely upon the business's economic results. For example, a bank wanting to enter the trust field will pay more for a trust company than IBM, which could not utilize the synergies that would accrue to the bank through its acquisition. Similarly, an accountant buying a real estate practice would not pay as much as another real estate agent who would obtain synergies by combining the two agencies. The valuator must be alert to the existence of any special purchasers and, when they are identified, must investigate the potential effect on value these buyers would have. For Canada Customs and Revenue Agency, fair market value does not take into account special purchasers unless they are clearly identified. For purposes of an ESOP synergistic purchasers should be considered very carefully and accounted for in the valuation.

Valuation Methodologies

There are a variety of valuation methods used to calculate a range of reasonable values. These methods can be broadly categorized into either asset-based or earnings-based approaches.

GOING CONCERN VERSUS LIQUIDATION

To assess which methodology to use, the question is whether the company is a going concern. The methodology used will depend on the answer. From a valuation perspective a going concern is a business that can continue to operate and produce products and services into the foreseeable future. The company has the following attributes:

- The ability to generate profits and cash flows in excess of expenses either currently or in the foreseeable future.

- It is not in bankruptcy or insolvency.

- It can meet its supplier and creditor obligations.

- It can collect its receivables in a normal fashion.

- It does not have material contingent liabilities or lawsuits which could create a bankrupt or insolvent company.

Some businesses are set up as holding companies and may have marginal profitability or losses. This does not exclude them from being classified as going concerns.

APPROACHES TO VALUE

The chart below summarizes the various approaches to value:

METHOD OF VALUE
IS THE COMPANY A GOING CONCERN

	Earnings-Based	Asset-Based
NO	LIQUIDATION VALUE	
YES	Capitalization of Earnings	Adjusted Asset Value
	Capitalization of Cash Flow	
	Discounted Cash Flow	

A "no" response results in a liquidation value. A "yes," however, results in two broad-based alternatives, a capitalization approach or an adjusted-asset approach and/or liquidation approach. Many valuators will use several approaches and then compare them. This allows the valuator to check his or her assumptions and reflect on any inconsistencies in the approaches.

METHODOLOGIES

There are basically two valuation approaches. One approach is dependent on asset values and the other on earnings. The earnings approach governs many going-concern circumstances because the worth of the company tends to be based on its future earnings. Assets can often comprise the value of a corporation where, because of industry influences and market conditions, the future for a company's earnings can be uncertain.

CAPITALIZATION OF EARNINGS

This model consists of three calculations: First, an estimate of the company's future maintainable earnings; second, the price/earnings multiple or multiplier (P/E multiple); and third, the value of identifiable redundant assets. The difficulty with this approach is knowing the appropriate capitalization rate or P/E multiple to use for a given company. P/E multiples are discussed later in the chapter.

Maintainable Earnings

In evaluating maintainable earnings it is important to understand the nature of the business cycle of the company being valued. An investor always purchases future earnings. The past is only an indicator of this future. Therefore, the risk inherent in every appraisal is estimating the quality and preservation of future cash flows.

Earnings quality is dependent upon two main factors:

- The expertise of key corporate management (including not only senior executives) but also key persons throughout the organization including technical, sales, and accounting staff.

- The product or service (including competitive advantages, business cycles, and market penetration).

In assessing key management, an organization chart detailing titles, responsibilities, ages, and length of employment is essential. This chart allows prompt identification of key persons who should be interviewed, as well as organizational weakness due to lack of qualified backup personnel.

The company's dependence on sales from any one individual or group of individuals should be determined. If the results show a material dependence, an investigation should be undertaken into whether these people are under contract, and what, if any, is their stake in staying with the company.

The importance of this review of key persons cannot be overstated. Consider the recent takeover by a large multi-national of a small regional competitor. The multi-national paid a high price for the company but due to different corporate cultures, several key sales persons with the regional competitor left within six months of the acquisition and took one-half of the sales volume. Had this risk been properly addressed, the buyer likely would not have paid such a high price.

The appraiser must also determine the nature of the company's product or service. Is the company in a cyclical industry and subject to severe volatility based on economic growth and recession? Are the products and services price-sensitive such that increased competition will tend to decrease profitability? Can the company maintain its unique market niche, which will protect premium prices in the marketplace?

Having reviewed the quality of future earnings, the appraiser then looks to its maintainability or, in service sector parlance, its retention factor. Are sales being maintained due to contractual obligation with clients? Or are they due to licenses, patents, or trademarks? What rate of new clients is generated each year? What rate of old clients is lost each year? Is the sales and earnings trend increasing or decreasing? A good example of the importance of the maintainability factor is in the accounting field. Generally an accounting practice will be purchased over a three-year period, and the purchase price will be reduced by the loss of client volume over that period (no retention, no value).

Price to Earnings Multiple (P/E)

The capitalization rate measures the rate of return required by an investor for an asset. Its inverse is the P/E multiple. For example, a required rate of return of 10 per cent on an asset equates to a P/E multiple of 10 (1 divided by 0.1), and a rate of return of 20 per cent equates to a P/E multiple of 5 (1 divided by 0.2).

Of the three components of value used in this model, the P/E multiple can be the most subjective element. Due to this subjectiveness, appraisers generally use a range of multiples to calculate value. Therefore, P/E multiples of four to five times are used rather than a single multiple of either four or five times.

The capitalization rate is a function of many risk-related variables:

- the quality and maintainability of future earnings;

- historical and current verbal or written offers for buying or selling stock in the company being valued;

- history of trading in stock of the company;

- shareholder buy-sell agreements' definition of value, possibly through a valuation formula;

- tangible asset backing such as real estate, machinery and equipment, patents;

- industry and country economic conditions;

- comparables of public stock and P/E multiples; and

- current market for closely held companies.

Assessing these factors is the art of appraising. Each factor can change the risk, which contributes to altering the capitalization rate. An investment such as a Canada bond paying, for example, 8 per cent provides a benchmark as to a risk-free rate of return. This risk-free rate of return defines the capitalization rate for a risk-free investment at 8 per cent. As risk increases due to various factors, the capitalization rate for the business increases as well.

Once the risk factors have been identified, a range of rates of return can be applied by the appraiser. These rates are then converted to their equivalent P/E multiples. An example of a build-up of a capitalization rate follows:

Risk free rate of return (long term Canada Bonds)	8%
Business risks including quality and maintainability of earnings	5–15%
Industry risk, including volatility of business cycle	5–10%
Rate of return required (8+5+5) to (8+15+10)	18–33%
P/E multiple (1/0.33 to 1/0.18)	3–5.6

Redundant Assets

Redundant assets are current and long-term assets such as cash, GICs, and term deposits, which are recorded on the books of the company but are not utilized in its day-to-day operations. Purchasers can withdraw these redundant assets without impairing the operations of the company. Therefore, these assets must be identified and added, net of appropriate income taxes, to the capitalization of earnings value.

For example, if a company is earning $1 million after tax, and a P/E multiple of five to six times is used, the capitalization of earnings value is $5 million to $6 million. Assume the same company has $1 million in GICs, which is not needed for working capital or for future capital expenditures. Withdrawing the $1 million from the company results in $350,000 in income tax and a redundant asset of $650,000, which, added to the earnings value, results in an overall value of ($5 to $6 million + $650,000) $5,650,000 to $6,650,000.

Redundant assets can be hidden through a company debt structure on the balance sheet. For example, a company with no long-term debt but a high asset value would be able to borrow against these assets. As long as the borrowing did not affect the operations or risk of the company, these borrowed assets could be withdrawn.

Privately held companies generally do not hold major redundant assets, which could disqualify the owner from claiming the $500,000 capital gains exemption on a disposition of their shares.

The capitalization of earnings model is the approach most often used in valuing going-concern privately held companies for ESOP purposes. However, like all valuation models, it has pitfalls for the unwary. Using a common-sense business analysis of the risks inherent in the target company will help avoid the pitfalls and arrive at a supportable value calculation.

CAPITALIZATION OF CASH FLOWS

This method is similar to the capitalization of earnings except in two respects. First, the cash flow method adds back non-cash expenses such as depreciation and amortization charges to arrive at the company's maintainable cash flows. Second, capital expenditures net of their tax shield (see below) are subtracted from the maintainable cash flows. Capital expenditures are those estimated capital costs that allow the company to maintain its forecast sales volume, for example, capital acquisition of buildings or machinery and equipment necessary to reduce higher forecast volumes.

The tax shield is the tax savings created by the capital cost allowance associated with the estimated capital expenditures. It is calculated as follows:

$$\frac{\text{Investment Cost (UCC)} \times \text{Rate of Income Tax} \times \text{Rate of CCA}}{\text{Rate of Return} + \text{Rate of Capital Cost Allowance}}$$

DISCOUNTED CASH FLOW

The discounted cash flow (DCF) method is used mainly for extractive industries, businesses that have a contractual basis for future sales volumes, or in high-growth industries such as knowledge-based industries.

This method calculates the net cash available over a time frame (usually three to 10 years) and presents values that cash back at a discount rate. For example, an engineering firm has created a new product and the estimated sales volume of the new product at approximately $100,000 per year with royalty from the product of 25 per cent after income tax. The company estimates that the royalty will increase by inflation rate of 6 per cent per annum. The amount of sales for this particular product will last approximately 10 years, generating in years approximately $1 million in sales.

The value using a DCF model would be calculated as follows:

Year	Sales	Royalty $	Present Value Factor at 10%	Present Value Factor 20%	Present Value at 10%	Present Value at 20%
1997	$100,000	85,000	.909	.833	77,265	70,805
1998	$100,000	90,100	.826	.694	74,423	62,529
1999	$100,000	95,506	.751	.579	71,725	55,298
2000	$100,000	101,236	.683	.482	69,144	48,796
2001	$100,000	107,311	.621	.402	66,640	43,139
2002	$100,000	113,749	.564	.335	64,154	38,106
2003	$100,000	120,574	.513	.279	61,854	33,640
2004	$100,000	127,809	.467	.233	59,687	29,779
2005	$100,000	135,477	.424	.194	57,442	26,283
2006	$100,000	143,606	.386	.162	55,432	23,264
					657,766	431,639

Therefore, the value of the royalty would be in the range of $432,000 to $658,000.

ASSET VALUES

The asset-based value approach is used when corporate assets do not earn a reasonable rate of return on their capital investment. This can happen when a company is showing a loss or is in a marginally profitable operation. If this situation is expected to continue, an asset-based approach may be appropriate. Under this approach, there are two methods, adjusted asset value and liquidation value.

Adjusted Asset Value

Under this method, the company is assumed to be a going concern. However, due to poor earnings or cash flow, its value is related to the potential sale of its net assets (assets minus liabilities).

To calculate value using this approach, each asset and liability is revalued to its fair market value. For assets such as land, buildings, machinery and equipment, one should look to expert appraisers.

Further adjustments to the net assets may arise due to contingent liabilities. Income tax due upon sale of land and depreciable assets is a major contingent cost. These costs include income taxes on capital gains and on recaptured depreciation. The full income tax payable may be used as a deduction from the net asset, or a portion thereof, or no deduction may be used, depending upon the facts of the situation. Other contingencies to be considered include lawsuits, tax reassessments, or warranties.

Liquidation Value

The liquidation value method assumes one of two value concepts: either that the company is not a going concern, or that the company is a going concern but has no expectation of future maintainable earnings or cash flow.

In either case, the net assets must be valued on their net realizable value. A forced liquidation approach assumes a quick sale, while an orderly liquidation approach assumes a sale over a reasonable period of time, not at rock-bottom prices.

The most common approach is an orderly liquidation. However, if there is a severe cash problem or the company cannot continue, a forced approach may be used. In the liquidation approach, all assets are assumed sold and income taxes paid. The result is a company holding only cash assets. At this point, the tax cost to distribute the cash assets out of the corporation must be calculated. The actual deduction can range from nil to the full tax cost. Many appraisers will take the midpoint for fairness to both the buyer and seller's position.

TAX SHIELD

It may be necessary to value depreciable property under the asset-based approach. This occurs because a purchaser buying a depreciable property inside a corporation loses the step up in the cost base out of the depreciable property. Therefore, the tax shield that is lost must be subtracted from the value of the property. This deduction should be made only in situations where the company is a going concern.

RULES OF THUMB

Rules of thumb tend to be used in industries that are service-oriented, and where there are few comparable publicly held companies. These special industries have, over time, developed rules of thumb for arriving at a company's value. Rules of thumb have several advantages. They can offer a method of comparing intra-industry transactions, price test the marketplace for that industry, give both buyer and seller insight into that industry, and highlight areas that may not have been valued previously. Finally, rules of thumb can test the reasonableness or lack of same, of each party's value analysis.

Rules of thumb should not be relied upon to the exclusion of proper financial analysis. The industry rule of thumb can be only a benchmark. It is an indication of what the market is likely to do in pricing the business, but if taken out of context, can lead to a extreme mispricing of the business. As well, rules of thumb change with time, and the use of an outdated rule can cause serious pricing problems. For example, radio stations are often traded on multiples of gross revenues plus net tangible assets. In the early 70s, these multiples would have ranged from two to over three times growth revenues. In the mid-80s, these multiples dropped to one to three times gross revenues. Of course using the wrong multiple could overvalue the purchase of a radio station in 2001. Other examples of industries with changing rules of thumb include: retailers based on square footage, auto leasing based on number of cars leased at $x per car, cable TV based on number of subscribers, newspapers based on number of subscribers, funeral homes based on annual numbers of funerals, and advertising and insurance agency firms based on gross commissions. The list is endless. Nevertheless rules of thumb in pricing are practical but only if used with extreme caution: the source must be reliable and the data must be current.

CORRELATION OF VALUES

Correlation of values is an important function because different methods use different assumptions. By computing value under several methods, the valuator can assess whether a material error has been made in the assumptions or the calculations. For example, an assessor may calculate the following results:

- capitalization of earnings approach $500,000,

- adjusted asset value $250,000, and

- rule of thumb $1,500,000.

Clearly, the valuator would need to do additional work to analyze why the rule of thumb was significantly different from the other approaches.

SANITY TESTS

Sanity tests or smell tests are useful for checking the overall reasonableness of the value. In the end, value is a range that must be based upon sound logic and common business sense. For example, a value for a knowledge-based company in the high tech field will in many cases exceed its sales revenue. Goodwill values in excess of five years in these areas may also require reevaluation. Current prices being paid for high-growth computer companies can be as high as two to eight times annual sales volumes.

Consequently, the valuator must always step back from the calculated value and ask: Is the company truly worth this value, and would I sign a cheque for this amount?

SHAREHOLDERS' AGREEMENTS

A shareholders' agreement is critical to creating liquidity for the employees in an ESOP, and the valuation element is crucial to the success of this document. Generally, there are three common approaches to calculating value for a shareholders' agreement. They are periodic independent valuation, fixed values, and formula.

Periodic Independent Valuation

For periodic independent valuation, parties hire an independent valuator to calculate the company's value at specific intervals, usually annually. Unfortunately, few business owners take this approach, mainly because of the perceived costs. Advantages of the periodic independent valuation approach are that

- It is based on the definition of fair market value.

- It is the fairest approach to be utilized by the employees.

- It reduces the possibility of disagreement with tax authorities.

The disadvantages are that

- It can be costly if the company is changing rapidly from year to year.

- The employees cannot easily calculate the company's value.

- There is no definite value for future funding arrangement.

Fixed Value

The shareholders themselves fix a value periodically, usually annually. Shareholders meet once a year and agree to the value of the company. This is formalized by signing a schedule to the agreement with the appropriate value indicated. For an ESOP the shareholders would be the original founding owners. The advantages of using fixed value are

- simplicity,

- certainty of value, and

- provision of value for funding.

The disadvantages are

- tax authorities may disagree,

- may not be fair to the employees,

- needs to be updated regularly, which unfortunately, is after the first few years, and

- potential source of shareholder disagreement.

Formula

The original shareholders define a formula that is used to value the shares annually. For example, the book value or multiple earnings may be used as a value. The advantages are

- no need for outside review,

- less expensive, and

- can be calculated in advance by employees.

The disadvantages are

- tax authorities may disagree,

- Can be unfair to the current shareholding group or to future employees,

- does not reflect changing business conditions.

VALUATION ISSUES IN A SHAREHOLDERS' AGREEMENT

Transaction Value

The original shareholders provide for a shotgun (put call) or right of first refusal within the agreement. Generally, these approaches always favour the stronger shareholder and may not be fair to the employees who are in the minority position.

Valuation date

The date of the valuation can be based on either the latest annual valuation or an interim valuation based on the latest quarter.

Minority Shareholder

How will minority shares be treated upon an employee's exit? Will the value of the shares be calculated by *pro rata en bloc* value or using a minority discount? A decision must also be made as to whether the minority discount will be in place if there is a actual third-party buyout.

Income taxes

A shareholders' agreement should address whether there should be full or partial calculation of contingent taxes.

Goodwill

Goodwill should be discussed in terms of calculations based on certain circumstances, such as retirement. The shareholders' agreement should indicate if there is to be no goodwill calculation. And the definition of goodwill value should be clearly stated, whether fair market value, or fair value, or fair price.

EMPLOYEE SHARE OWNERSHIP PLANS AND SPECIAL VALUATION ISSUES

One of the most pressing problems for business owners is finding a way to liquify their equity in a business into cash for retirement or other purposes. However, their decision to sell is often more than an economic one. A founding owner develops a strong feeling of identity with the company and a strong sense of loyalty to the employees. In many cases, the owner would like the employees to have a role in the business through an ESOP.

- Will the sales to arms'-length employees be at fair market value or below fair market value? Either may give rise to personal income tax consequences.

- Will the sales to non-arms'-length employees come under the Canada Customs and Revenue Agency's scrutiny?

- Will the valuation be performed by an independent party knowledgeable in business appraisals so as to create the level of trust with the employees that is critical to the success of the ESOP?

- If additional debt is being acquired by the company to leverage a sale to the employees, what is the impact of this additional debt on the value of the company?

- What minority discount will apply to ESOP shares, and what are the terms and conditions in the buy-sell agreement that will relate to that minority discount?

MAXIMIZING SHAREHOLDER VALUE

All business people know how to package, market, and sell their products and services. Few, however, know how to package, market, and sell their company. This is critical for the ESOP because the employees need a liquidity event to generate the wealth in their investment in the company. Employees need to know how to increase the company's value so the company and its stakeholders will succeed. The following issues should be evaluated in readying a company for sale.

IMPROVING FINANCIAL POSITION

Before selling a company, financial preparatory work is essential. However, personal tax-planning needs must be considered before implementing any of the actions suggested in the following paragraphs.

Balance Sheet

Up to two years prior to selling, any weaknesses inherent in the company's balance sheet should be addressed. A company's value can be enhanced through improving the strength of its balance sheet. Detailed ratio analysis comparing industry norms to company norms and identifying areas for improvement should be made. In addition, improving liquidity ratios by reducing outstanding accounts receivable improve the company's balance sheet. A liquidity ratio defines the company's cash flow and determines whether the company has sufficient short-term cash flow to be able to continue operations and provide for expansion. The company should remove all non-operating assets through a tax advantage basis, for example, term deposits. Any non-operating loans that are within the company should be reduced if possible. If the company intends to acquire new technology to create production efficiencies, this should be done before the company is put up for sale. Any contingent liabilities such as lawsuits or past tax issues should be cleared up. Inventory costing, which can impact the profitability of the company, should be stabilized for a number of years.

Earning Statement

The earning statement can be improved in several areas, which will help the company in terms of its value and in terms of its saleability. Again, a ratio analysis to compare company results and industry norms will identify areas of weakness. The company should reduce non-operating and non-recurring expenses and keep them to a minimum. In addition, the company should start reducing payments to any family and spouses who are not involved in the company. This should be done in any event once an ESOP plan is put into place. The company should reduce excessive interest costs by a commitment to reduce loans outstanding. If there are long-term leases coming due and the company is dependent on its location, these long-term leases should be taken care of. Any bad debts that have been accrued due to improper credit controls should be corrected.

Administration

It is very important that the company have its financial records reviewed on a regular basis. Being able to provide monthly financial statements indicates to potential buyers that the company had its books in order. Any banking relationships that are not sound should be made so as soon as possible, and the company must ensure that its year-end financials are available within a reasonable time period (preferably six weeks of the year-end).

Strengthen Key Management

One of the key value components of any company is its management team. When calculating the company's value, buyers will always consider the management team of the company and how long that management team has been with the company. Management positions should have trained backup personnel for all key areas in sales production and finance. The company should also put into place a comprehensive compensation package which to reward high-achieving key persons. An outside consultant can help with these training and compensation issues. Creating a board of directors with outside expertise can be very valuable in identifying potential purchasers. Buyers are comforted by the knowledge that the company has an experienced board of directors.

REDUCE INDUSTRY AND COMPANY RISK

There are many ways to reduce industry and company risk. The company should identify its key products and services and assess their long-term potential. In terms of the market curve, are corporate products and services at the beginning of that curve or at the end, and should new products be introduced? The company should plan for the introduction of any new products and services so that the process is underway. Increasing sales to a wider variety of customers will increase a company's value. If a company sells 90 per cent of its sales or services to a single customer, the company's value is reduced because the loss of that single customer would be catastrophic. The company should also ensure that it has at least two or three key suppliers for each major raw material required and that several sub-contractor groups are used.

CONVERT PERSONAL GOODWILL INTO COMMERCIAL GOODWILL

As we have said, commercial goodwill has value while personal good-will does not. Therefore, the company should ensure that long-term contracts with customers or suppliers are in place. Any patents or trademarked products or services that have not yet been marketed should be, to give substance and increase value. Any brand products or services in the marketplace should be identified, and key management must be under contract.

SELLING CYCLE

There is a time to sell every business. Having one's house in order does not mean that value will be maximized; the best time to sell is usually when mergers and acquisitions of large companies are in an upswing. Another good signal to sell is a strong stock market, especially for small-capitalization companies, which are valued at less than $250 million. Another good time to sell is after the economy has been growing for several years following a downturn; this tends to create the desire for acquisitions. Lastly, when market activity for small and medium-size companies is strong, demand will tend to increase a company's value.

TAX PLANNING

Because of the high income taxes in Canada it is critical to have proper tax planning before any efforts are made to increase the value of the company. Therefore, some of the following step should be considered. The company should ensure that it is a CCPC and that it is eligible for the $500,000 capital gains exemption. At the same time, it should merge or consolidate subsidiaries to help create a sale situation allows a con-solidated view of the company for potential purchasers.

CONCLUSION

Good business appraisals reflect sound valuation techniques as well as good common business sense. Someone once said that the only prob-lem with common sense is that it is not too common. This chapter has given the reader an overview of the valuation technique involved in ESOPs. The application of common sense is up to the reader. Once the business valuation issue has been resolved, the next key technical area is income tax, the subject of the next chapter.

ESOPs and Income Tax

INCOME TAXES ARE CRITICALLY IMPORTANT in Canada, and any ESOP plan, whether an equity plan, option plan, or phantom plan, must be tax effective for employees, owners, and future shareholders. The design parameters of the ESOP will, therefore, impose certain income tax implications for the plan participants. Likewise, specific tax laws can influence decisions on the design and structure of an ESOP. This chapter discusses Canadian income tax implications including

- types of participation,
- methods of ownership,
- financing,
- taxation of dividends,
- treatment of capital gains and losses,
- disposition of shares,
- going public,

- corporate deductions for ESOPs,

- Canadian Controlled Private Corporation (CCPC) status, and

- salary deferral arrangements.

1. Types of Participation

   As stated in earlier chapters, there are three common types of employee participation in an ESOP: stock purchases (share equity), stock options, and phantom shares. In addition, share appreciation rights (SARs) are a less frequently used form of participation. An ESOP may involve one type of participation exclusively or a combination. For example, a combination of stock purchase and stock options is often used to ensure that the employees both have invested their own funds and also have an additional incentive at no additional cost through the stock options.

2. Methods of Ownership

   There are three possible methods of ownership of ESOP shares. They are direct personal ownership, ownership through RRSPs and ownership through a holding company. There are a number of factors that affect the method of ownership.

3. Financing

   As discussed previously, there are many methods for employees to finance the acquisition of shares in a company. These range from having the employees using their own funds, or borrowing funds from institutions, friends, family, or the company, to the use of corporate bonuses or their RRSPs.

4. Taxation of Dividends

   Depending upon the specifics of the plan, dividends may be payable upon certain types of shares offered to employees. Dividends will come from several sources. If an employee has direct ownership of the shares, any dividends declared on that class of shares will be paid to that employee based on the percentage of shares that he or she owns. If the employee had purchased the shares through an RRSP, dividends would be credited to the RRSP account.

5. Treatment of Capital Gains and Losses

   One of the key benefits of owning shares in a company is the ability to generate gains that would be taxed as capital gains rather than as income, income tax rates on personal income being much higher than capital gains rates. The rules and regulations, however, are very specific in this area and require that the plan achieve the best after-tax effects for the employee.

6. Disposition of Shares

   The employee will want to dispose of his or her shares. It is at this liquidity event where the employee can increase their wealth. There are several ways in which shares can be disposed of. The company can be bought out by a third party, in which case the employee would then share in any gain on the sale to that third party. The company itself could buy back the shares from the employee, thus triggering certain income taxes, which will be discussed later. Another option that many companies take is to go public or to start an initial public offering (IPO). In this case, shares held by employees have certain restrictions on them that will allow employees to maximize their after-tax benefits.

7. Going Public

   A company that goes public is by definition no longer a CCPC. Therefore, steps must be taken to minimize the tax impact on employees.

8. Corporate Deductions for ESOPs

   There is limited income tax applicability for ESOPs in Canada as has been described earlier, but there are some tax implications that will be discussed in a more general format.

9. Canadian Controlled Private Corporation (CCPC) Status

   The CCPC status is very important so the employees can achieve the tremendous tax advantages that still exist under the *Income Tax Act*. Again, the plan must be put together properly so as to achieve these results.

10. Salary Deferral Arrangement

In any ESOP arrangement it is necessary to ensure that the plan does not qualify as a salary deferral arrangement (SDA), which will result in unanticipated tax consequences. An SDA is an arrangement where an employee has a right to receive an amount after one year. The main purpose of the arrangement is to postpone tax otherwise payable on salary in the year or previous year. But there are certain statutory exemptions to SDAs. The chapter will now discuss, in more detail, the income tax implications when a plan is put into place.

TYPES OF PARTICIPATION

Stock Purchase

In a stock purchase–type of ESOP, employees purchase shares from the company treasury and, in some cases, from the owners. The major difference between these types of acquisitions is that when an employee purchases shares from the treasury, the number of shares in the company increase and, therefore, the existing shareholders are diluted. When shares are purchased from the current owners, those owners, rather than the company, receive the funds. The maximum number of shares that each eligible employee can acquire is usually determined by a formula developed for the plan. For a cash purchase from treasury, the employee would pay the employer fair market value on the specified acquisition date for the shares. This amount will become the employee's adjusted cost base (ACB) of the shares used by the Canada Customs and Revenue Agency to calculate any capital gains that the employee may have to pay in future.

If the Canada Customs and Revenue Agency decided that the fair market value at the time of acquisition was actually higher than the subscription price (the price paid by the employee), the difference between the two would be considered an employment stock option benefit. The section of this chapter on the employment benefit deals with the taxation of this benefit. The amount of any such benefit would be added to the subscription price to determine the employee's ACB of the shares. In other words, the employee, when selling his shares at some future event, will have to pay increased taxes. From the employer's perspective, the subscription price would be added to the paid-up capital (PUC) of the class of shares utilized. Where a stock option benefit occurs, there is not a PUC addition for that amount, and no deduction is available to the employer.

Stock Options

The granting of options to an employee has no immediate tax consequences for the employee, but the terms of the options granted will have future tax consequences. The employee may be entitled to deductions of 50 per cent of any employment benefit realized.

To qualify for this deduction, the employer must be a Canadian-controlled private corporation (CCPC) and the employee must deal at arm's length after the option is granted. Also, the employee must hold onto the shares for two years, although an exception is made when there is a deemed disposition on death. If qualifying employees of a CCPC do not hold their shares for the two-year period, they will still be entitled to the deduction if the tests for other employers are met. If a CCPC employer goes public or sells out to a non-resident, the deferred employment benefits do not immediately become taxable because it is the corporation's status at the time the option is granted that is relevant for taxation purposes.

Employment Benefit

When the fair market value is greater than the amount paid for the shares under the option, the difference is considered a benefit by virtue of employment and, therefore, is taxed in the same manner as salary, wages, or other remuneration in the taxation year in which the option is exercised. However, for the shares of a CCPC, the benefit and resulting employment income is deferred until the employee disposes of the shares. Transfer of the shares to a registered retirement savings plan (RRSP) is considered a sale for taxation purposes. This issues is discussed in "Ownership through RRSPs" on page 103.

The February 28, 2000 Federal Budget proposed amendments to the above tax treatment for employees of a non-CCPC. A brief summary of the budget proposals, based on the draft legislation in respect thereof tabled on December 21, 2000, is as follows:

- The budget proposals are available for stock options exercised after February 27, 2000. These proposals apply regardless of when the option was granted or became vested in the employee.

- All or a portion of the taxable benefit in respect of the stock option may be deferred from the year of acquisition of the shares to the year in which the shares are sold if certain criteria are met.

- The deferral will not be available unless the exercise price under the option was the fair market value of the share when the option was granted. The security also must be listed on a prescribed stock exchange either in Canada or outside of Canada (prescribed stock exchanges include the TSE, NYSE, and NASDAQ). There are rules to prevent the conversion of an option for an unlisted security to an option for a listed security.

- The shares acquired must be prescribed shares. Generally, prescribed shares are ordinary common shares.

- The employee must deal at arm's length with the employer immediately after the option is granted.

- The employee must be resident in Canada at the time the shares are acquired.

- The deferral is available to a maximum of $100,000 of security value vested per year. The security value is based on the value of the security at the time the options are granted. However, there are no restrictions on how many of the vested options can be exercised in any given year.

- The deferral is not available for an employee who is a "specified shareholder" at the time the option was granted. A "specified shareholder" means a taxpayer who, along with non-arm's length parties, owns 10 per cent or more of the shares of any class of the corporation. This restriction applies to shareholders of the employer, the corporation granting the option or the corporation whose shares could be acquired under the option.

- The employee must elect in prescribed form to defer the stock option benefit. If the election is not made, the benefit will be taxable at the time the option is exercised.

- The employer will have to report deferred stock option benefits on the employee's T4 for the year in which the shares are acquired. The onus will be on the employee to report deferred benefits on their tax return for the year in which the shares are solds.

Any employment income realized as above is added to the option price paid to arrive at the employee's ACB for income tax purposes. The ACB is not reduced for the 50 per cent deduction noted above since there is no applicable provision in the act. From the employer's perspective, the option price is added to the paid-up capital of the class of shares utilized for the ESOP. There is no deduction available to the employer.

Capital Gains Exemption

An employee might want to exercise the option to obtain ownership of the shares, even if an immediate sale is not planned. For example, due to the restrictions inherent in an Initial Public Offering (IPO), it may not be possible to sell the shares right away. Also, in order to obtain the $500,000 capital gains exemption on a capital gain resulting from a sale of the shares, the employee must hold them for at least two years. Therefore, the employee might wish to obtain current ownership of the shares to be able to use the exemption on a future sale. In addition, current ownership may be desirable for tax planning purposes in the event that the employer were to become a public company or cease to be a small business corporation (SBC). Where the employer is paying dividends on the class of shares, the employee might wish to exercise the options in order to be able to receive dividends. However, not all companies will pay dividends, as the equity may be required for the growth of the business.

Disposition of Option Rights

An employee may be in the position to effectively dispose of the option rights by receiving cash instead of shares in settlement of the option rights. When an employee has the right to elect to receive cash instead of shares, the cash received is included in income as a stock option benefit, and the employee would be able to obtain the 50 per cent deduction, provided the conditions discussed above are met. The employer would get a deduction for the amount paid, since shares were not sold or issued to the employees. When it is at the employer's discretion to offer a cash payment, the payment then is considered regular employment income. The employee is therefore not entitled to the 50 per cent deduction, but the employer can claim a deduction for the payment made.

If an employee who has stock options becomes a non-resident of Canada, the deemed disposition rules on departure do not apply to the stock option. Canada retains the right to tax the taxable benefit, if any, realized on exercise of the options. Where the emigrant employee holds CCPC shares acquired under a stock option, the shares are deemed disposed of on departure. However, the fair market value proceeds on the deemed disposition will be reduced by the amount of the stock option benefit that will be taxed in Canada on the eventual disposition of the shares. In addition, the stock option benefit for shares of a CCPC remains deferred.

Phantom Plans

Phantom plans do not involve issuing any shares to employees. Rather, phantom plans involve payments to employees by the employer that are tied to share value appreciation and any dividends that would have been paid on shares issued. In a typical phantom plan, an employee is granted a notional number of shares in the company. After a set period of time, the employee may dispose of these notional shares. On such a disposition, an amount is paid by the employer to the employee equal to any increase in the fair market value of the notional shares over the holding period.

As a phantom plan does not involve an agreement to sell or issue shares, the stock option provisions do not apply. In addition, the payment by the employer for the fair market value increase in the notional shares would be taxable to the employee as employment income, not as a capital gain or as a dividend. The employer would get a deduction for the amount of the payment made to the employee under the phantom plan.

Share Appreciation Rights

Share appreciation rights (SARs) are a variation on the phantom plan concept but tied to stock options as opposed to notional shares. With SARs, the employee obtains the benefits of a stock option without exercising the option. The employee has the option of exercising either the share appreciation rights or the underlying stock option. For example, if an employee had a share appreciation right, and the stock increased in value, the employee can notify the company that he or she is exercising the stock appreciation right and get the benefit or the increase of the value rather than going through the stock option methodology. Most SARs are used in public companies or in larger private companies. If the share appreciation rights are exercised, the employee receives a cash payment from the employer in the amount of the difference between the fair market value of the stock and the option price.

From the employee's perspective the payment is treated as a stock option benefit. The employee may also be eligible for the 50 per cent deduction, provided the conditions for qualification are met. From the employer's perspective, a deduction is claimed for the amount of the cash payment made to the employee. There are thus tax benefits to both parties. For SARs to be workable, there must be a method to quickly turn them into cash, which is why SARs are suitable mainly in public companies that can be traded on the stock market.

METHODS OF OWNERSHIP

Direct Personal Ownership

There are a number of reasons why employees might consider direct ownership of ESOP shares rather than holding them through an RRSP. If funds from dividends or the sale of the shares will be required for personal use, direct personal ownership would be the appropriate alternative. The $500,000 capital gains exemption is available only with personal ownership. Thus, if the company qualifies for the exemption, personal ownership may be advisable. The preferential tax treatment on capital gains (50 per cent inclusion rate) and capital dividends are lost where shares are held through the employee's RRSP, as all amounts are fully taxable when withdrawing from the RRSP.

Ownership through RRSPs

If funds derived from the ESOP shares are intended for retirement and are not currently needed, an employee may wish to consider holding ESOP shares in an RRSP. This would defer the tax on any dividends or capital gains until such time as funds are withdrawn from the RRSP. An eligible employee can establish a self-directed RRSP to hold the ESOP shares at any financial institution. An employee who wishes to own his or her ESOP shares in an RRSP must put them into a self-directed plan.

Qualified Investments

If the employer is a Canadian public corporation it is likely that the shares will be qualified for an RRSP. However, shares of a foreign corporation are restricted in quantity available to be invested in the RRSP. There are additional restrictions on investments in CCPCs by an RRSP. The regulations to the act allow an RRSP to purchase shares of an eligible corporation including those that meet the same test as for a small business corporation (SBC), as long as the annuitant under the RRSP is not related to the corporation and holds (including shares held by non-arms-length persons) less than 10 per cent of any class of shares of the company. If the employee, owning the RRSP and other non-arms-length persons are to own 10 per cent or more of any class of shares of the company, the cost of the investment by the RRSP must be less than $25,000. The SBC test must be met either at the time the RRSP makes the share investment or at the prior fiscal year end of the company. Employees who will own less than 10 per cent of any class of shares and are purchasing their shares for cash may wish to consider using their RRSP to make the investment, if they have available contribution limits or funds available in their RRSP. It should be noted that subsequent investments outside the RRSP that put the combined shareholdings at 10 per cent or more will not disqualify investments already in the RRSP. An RRSP can own stock options. Shares could also be transferred to an RRSP after acquisition by the employee under the stock option.

Transfer of Shares to an RRSP

Contributions to an RRSP may be in cash or in kind, and there is nothing to stop employees from holding ESOP shares in their RRSP. Provided the shares are a qualified investment for an RRSP as described above, a tax deduction may be claimed for the fair market value of the shares contributed, subject to the normal contribution limits. This assumes that the RRSP does not pay for the shares out of cash already in the RRSP but that the shares are a contribution to the RRSP. The deduction is subject to the normal contribution limits, but any excess may be carried forward to apply against future RRSP limits.

The employee would be considered to have sold his or her shares at fair market value at the time of the contribution to the RRSP. Any resulting capital gain would be taxable to the employee, the $500,000 exemption would offset the gain if the shares qualified for the exemption. Should a capital loss arise, it would not be deductible to the employee. Consequently, it is generally not advisable to transfer shares with significant accrued losses to an RRSP. Any employment benefit not previously taxed would become subject to tax at the time of transfer. The transfer of the shares also triggers the taxable benefit if the benefit was previously deferred. The section of this chapter on the employment benefit deals with this issue.

In considering whether or not the ESOP investment should be made through an RRSP, the employee should consider all aspects of personal financial planning, including the overall asset mix of the RRSP.

STRATEGIES FOR THE $500,000 CAPITAL GAINS EXEMPTION

Whether the ESOP shares would be eligible for the $500,000 exemption, there are difficulties in determining whether or not the shares should be held in the employee's RRSP. For example, assume an employee has acquired 5,000 shares at $1.00 per share (current fair market value), under a share purchase ESOP. The employee then contributes the shares to his or her RRSP. The shares would have an ACB to the employee and a fair market value of $5,000. Thus, there would be no capital gain or loss on the transfer, and the employee would get an RRSP deduction of $5,000 but would use up $5,000 of the employee's RRSP contribution limit. If the RRSP later sells the shares for $100,000, the gain of $95,000 would be sheltered. There would be no $500,000 exemption available because the RRSP, not the employer, sold the shares. On retirement, the withdrawal of the $100,000 would be fully taxable.

In the opposite scenario, assume that the employee did not initially contribute the shares to the RRSP. Two years after acquisition, the shares have a fair market value of $2.00 per share or $10,000 in total and are eligible for the $500,000 exemption. If the employee were now to contribute the shares to the RRSP, there would be a capital gain of $5,000 ($10,000 fair market value minus $5,000 ACB) which would be offset by the $500,000 exemption. The employee would have an RRSP deduction of $10,000 and use up $10,000 of his or her RRSP contribution limit. If the RRSP later sells the shares for $100,000, the gain of $90,000 would be sheltered. There would be no $500,000 exemption available because, again, the RRSP, not the individual, sold the shares. On retirement, the withdrawal of the $100,000 would again be fully taxable. Thus the only advantage in waiting the two years to contribute the shares to the RRSP is to use the $500,000 exemption to increase the amount of RRSP contribution if the employee does not wish to use other funds to contribute to the RRSP. The employee has effectively utilized the capital gains exemption to shelter the capital gain which allows for the higher RRSP contribution. If the value increases significantly during the two-year period, the employee may have insufficient RRSP contribution room to contribute all the shares.

Ownership Through a Holding Company

It is possible for employees to own ESOP shares through a holding company. Where a share purchase ESOP is involved, the purchase could be made directly by the holding company. Where stock options are involved, the employee would first exercise the option and then transfer the shares to the holding company. It appears that there would potentially be no capital gain on this transfer as any stock option benefit would be added to the ACB of the shares. The stock option benefit is deemed to have been received in the applicable taxation year and is subject to tax. The amount of the benefit is added to the ACB of the shares.

There are a number of disadvantages to holding the shares through a holding company. The $500,000 exemption is available only to individuals and when the shares are to be sold the holding company, rather than the employee would be selling the shares. If the employer company is a qualifying SBC at the time of sale, the benefit of the exemption would be lost unless the employee is able to sell the holding company shares. In addition, the holding company would itself have to be a qualifying SBC and connected with the employer. If the employer company is a CCPC with which the employee deals at arm's length, the deferral of any stock option benefit would be lost if the shares were transferred to a holding company after exercise of the option. Thus, a holding company would be a viable alternative in only limited circumstances for significant minority or majority shareholders, for income tax and/or estate planning purposes.

FINANCING

Borrowing

If an employee borrows to buy ESOP shares, interest on the borrowing is tax-deductible as long as the shares are held personally. However, interest on money borrowed to make an RRSP contribution is non-deductible.

Shares in Lieu of Bonuses

Some ESOPs are structured to allow employees to receive their shares in lieu of bonuses. It is essential that these bonuses not be considered merely an indirect payment of employment income known as "constructively received." Constructive receipt is considered to occur in situations where the employee has an absolute right to a payment or an amount is credited to an employee's account, set apart for the employee, or otherwise made available to the employee. The decision by the employee to receive shares in lieu of bonus must be made by the employee prior to the bonus being determined and declared by the employer to avoid the application of constructive receipt. The employee must not have an absolute right to the bonus or have the bonus determined and available for his or her use.

Companies use different methodologies for their bonus plans; each situation should be reviewed independently to ensure there is not constructive receipt of the bonus. Consideration could be given to the employees deciding to accept shares in lieu of bonus prior to the beginning of the year where the bonus is earned.

Should the bonus entitlement being used for shares be insufficient to cover the acquisition value of the shares, the employee would be required to fund the difference in cash. This financing option allows an arm's-length employee of the CCPC to defer tax that would otherwise be payable on a cash bonus. As mentioned previously, employers are not entitled to a deduction for the value of the shares issued, but they would have been entitled to a deduction for the payment of a cash bonus.

The receipt of shares in lieu of a bonus is taxed as a stock option with a zero exercise price. The section of this chapter on employment benefit deals with this issue.

RRSPs

As discussed, an employee's RRSPs can be used to finance his or her ESOP shares. Funds available in the RRSP can be utilized to acquire the shares under a share purchase ESOP, assuming that the shares otherwise qualify.

TAXATION OF DIVIDENDS

Direct Ownership

Dividends received on ESOP shares held personally will be included in investment income of the employee. These dividends would be taxed under the normal gross-up and dividend tax credit rules paid by any Canadian private or public company. The maximum marginal tax rate on taxable dividends will vary depending upon the employee's province of residence.

RRSP

Dividends received in an RRSP are taxable as ordinary income only when funds are withdrawn. The maximum marginal tax rate on ordinary income will vary depending upon the employee's province of residence.

TREATMENT OF CAPITAL GAINS AND LOSSES

Where shares are held personally, 50 per cent of any taxable capital gain is included in computing the individual's income for tax purposes. The $500,000 lifetime capital gains exemption on gains realized from the sale of qualifying SBC shares may be available to offset gains. Employees who have not fully used this exemption in the past should be aware of the following points:

- The exemption is available only for shares owned by individuals, not shares held in RRSPs.

- If the company eventually repurchases shares under buy-back provisions of an ESOP, any gain will likely be taxed primarily as a dividend, not as a capital gain, and thus the exemption would not be available. A capital loss is also usually realized.

- If someone other than the company purchases employee shares, the exemption may be available if the company is a qualified SBC at the time of sale.

- The use of the exemption may cause the employee to have alternative minimum tax. Minimum tax is a calculation required by Canada Customs and Revenue Agency to ensure that Canadians pay a minimum level of tax.

- If the employee has a (cumulative) net investment loss or has made previous claims for allowable business investment losses, the full exemption may not be available. A cumulative net investment loss is the result of past year investment losses which exceed investment income.

The definition of a qualified SBC share is quite complex, but in essence a SBC share is a CCPC that meets three tests:

- the shareholder has held the shares for at least 24 months prior to the sale;

- the company meets a 50 per cent active business asset test (on a fair market value basis) throughout the 24 months prior to sale; and the active business is carried out primarily in Canada; and

- the company meets a 90 per cent active business asset test (on a fair market value basis) at the time of sale.

Full review of the capital gains exemption rules is beyond the scope of this publication. Owners of companies are encouraged to consult their tax accountants to see whether they qualify under these rules.

Shares held personally can benefit from the $500,000 capital gains exemption, but shares held in an RRSP do not qualify for the exemption. Although any capital gain realized in an RRSP is not taxable, this is only a deferral, not an exemption, as funds are fully taxable when withdrawn from the RRSP. One hundred per cent of the gain is included in the income versus 50 per cent if the shares are held outside the RRSP.

DISPOSITION OF SHARES

Sale

On a sale of the ESOP shares to anyone other than the company, an employee will generally realize a capital gain or loss. A gain will arise if the sale proceeds exceed the cost of the shares plus any costs of disposal. A loss will be realized if the sale of proceeds is less than the cost of the shares plus any costs of disposal. In some cases, such as a transfer of shares to an RRSP, any loss will be denied. Any employment benefit not taxed at the time a stock option is exercised will be recognized at the time of sale, as indicated above.

Buyback of Shares

There may be circumstances defined in an ESOP in which an employee may be required to sell his or her shares back to the company. In these buy-back circumstances, the employee will be considered for tax purposes to have received the dividend equal to the difference between the proceeds and the paid-up capital (PUC) of the shares. This is why it is important to know the PUC of the shares. Capital gain or loss would also be realized, equal to the difference between the ACB and the PUC of the shares. The dividend and any capital gain will be subject to tax. A capital loss will be deductible only against capital gains from other sources, unless the company is a SBC at the time of the buy back. This could result in current income for tax purposes and a capital loss carryover even though no economic gain has occurred. If the company is a SBC at the time of buy back, the loss may qualify as an allowable business investment loss (ABIL) and, as such, a portion of the loss may be deductible from income from all sources. Prior use of the capital gains exemption reduces the ability to claim the ABIL treatment. The PUC of a share is the average of the total PUC of all the shares of the particular class. Shares acquired in lieu of bonus entitlements will not result in any additions to the total PUC of the shares, as described above. PUC additions on shares acquired under stock options may be less than the ACB of the shares so acquired. Consequently, the ACB of an employee's shares will be in excess of the PUC thereof. Thus, employees may realize a dividend and a capital loss under the buy back provisions of the ESOP.

For example, assume an employee paid $1.00 per share, the PUC is 1 cent per share, and the shares are bought back for $1.50 per share. The employee would have a deemed dividend of $1.49 per share which would be included in income. The employee would also have a capital loss of $0.99 per share, which would be deductible only against capital gains from other sources, unless the company is an SBC at the time of the buyback. Assuming the employee cannot currently use the capital loss, tax would be paid on the deemed dividend. Any capital loss would be carried forward and would be available to offset capital gains.

This result could be avoided if the company deemed it appropriate to have the employee sell the shares to another employee as opposed to back to the company. The first alternative results in tax savings on the proceeds. Generally, the employee is significantly better off if the shares are sold to another employee rather than bought back. Savings would be even greater if the shares were eligible for the $500,000 capital gains exemption. In order to avoid adverse tax consequences, consideration could be given to having a separate company or a holding company that would purchase ESOP shares from employees, rather than having the employer buy back the shares. Reselling them to employees entering the plan can effectively act as a clearing house for ESOP shares.

Consideration could also be given to using a class of shares separate from that of the original owners for the ESOP. This would avoid some of the PUC averaging concerns, particularly where the principal owners have a large number of shares issued for a nominal amount. The principal owners would have a class of shares with high fair market value and nominal PUC, whereas the ESOP participants would have a second class of shares with a lower value and a comparatively high PUC. In considering this type of structure, the related legal and business issues should be evaluated. This approach would require careful communication to employees, explaining why they are receiving another class of shares.

GOING PUBLIC

Many ESOPs are started in private companies that later go public and, by definition, are no longer CCPCs. As such, gains on shares realized after going public would not be eligible for the $500,000 capital gains exemption. The act contains special provisions that would allow the employee to elect to recognize some or all of the gains realized up to the date of the IPO.

The election is available where an individual owns shares of a SBC that becomes a public company listed on a prescribed stock exchange. The shares are deemed disposed of for proceeds of disposition at the amount the shareholder elects. This elected amount can be anywhere between the ACB and the fair market value of the shares. Thus, the amount of gain realized can be fixed so as to only utilize the amount of capital gains exemption available. This deemed disposition will not trigger the recognition of any deferred stock option benefit. The shareholder is deemed to have re-acquired the shares at the elected amount. Thus, the gain realized is effectively added to the ACB of the shares for tax purposes. This means that the employee has been able to boost the

ACB of his or her stock, reducing the amount of taxes that he would normally pay.

CORPORATE DEDUCTIONS FOR ESOPS

In general, where a corporation has granted stock options to employees, there is no deduction for the employer for the benefit realized by the employee. Under common law, payments made to employees for acquiring shares of the employer from third parties are taxed as employment income in the employee's hands.

CANADIAN CONTROLLED PRIVATE CORPORATION STATUS

In order to meet the definition of CCPC, the company must qualify as a private company under the relevant securities legislation. For example, under the *Ontario Securities Act*, the company's articles must restrict the number of shareholders to 50 exclusive of (current) employees and former employees who were shareholders while employed by the company and continue to be so. The articles must also contain the standard clause prohibiting sale of the shares to the public. Consequently, the company's status as a private company could be jeopardized if more than 50 employees utilize their RRSP to hold the shares.

A company may also be designated a public company where

- A class of the corporation shares is qualified for distribution to the public.

- There are no fewer than 150 shareholders of any equity shares class, and 300 shareholders in any other class.

- Insiders hold not more than 80 per cent of the issue of outstanding shares of that class.

A CCPC status is required for both the deferral of stock option benefits and the $500,000 exemption, so the factors listed must be taken into account to ensure CCPC status is maintained.

SALARY DEFERRAL ARRANGEMENTS

As stated previously, in any ESOP it is necessary to ensure that the plan does not qualify as a salary deferral arrangement (SDA). A SDA is a plan where an employee has a right to receive an amount of salary after the year is complete. One of the main purposes of the arrangement is to postpone tax otherwise payable. There are certain statutory exceptions to SDAs.

An SDA can potentially apply to phantom stock plans, which would cause negative tax consequences to the employees. However, a prescribed plan or arrangement is exempt from SDA treatment. The requirements of a prescribed plan or arrangement are beyond the scope of this book. However, it is important to note that the SDA must be taken into account when setting up the plan so as to prevent negative tax consequences to both the employees and the employer. The best way to do this is to consult qualified tax counsel when putting the plan into place.

CONCLUSION

ESOPs are an integral component of compensation for employees in all types of industries in Canada. The income tax issues discussed above provide a general analysis of many of the key factors. These should be reviewed in depth when designing and structuring an ESOP. It is very important to the success of the plan that all tax factors are reviewed and researched thoroughly because the impact that income taxes have on the company, its value, and the ability of employees to create wealth is enormous. Key elements that have to be addressed in any kind of tax analysis are the tax positions of the various stakeholders, the current ownership group, the employees, and the company. It is important to know if any restructuring has to take place in any one of these groups to be able to create a proper tax plan. Another issue that has to be clarified is whether or not the company qualifies for the $500,000 tax exemption as well as capital gains treatment as this has a major impact on the employees' wealth creation. To address all these issues it is important that the best tax advice be obtained. In the end, however, no investment should be undertaken solely for tax purposes.

Since the goal of all ESOPs is to increase the wealth of each employee, it is important that the employees understand that the best tax planning must of course, be based on what optimizes the company's business and related value. Consequently, some of the tax planning techniques discussed in this chapter may not be available in a particular situation due to the business considerations. In terms of an investment vehicle, investing in their own company has advantages over alternative forms of investment, not the least of which is the power to influence the growth in value. The next chapter discusses the legal issues involved in designing an ESOP.

ESOP Legal Requirements

L<small>EGAL REQUIREMENTS</small> of an ESOP, whether a share equity, stock option, or phantom plan, are complex and detailed. Each ESOP has its own format and requires its own set of legal considerations both during the pre-ESOP stage and the post-ESOP stage. This chapter provides an overview of the types of plans and the legal issues that will arise depending upon each plan's unique objectives.

DIFFERENT OBJECTIVES—DIFFERENT LEGAL IMPLICATIONS

Each company has different objectives in its ESOP, thereby ensuring that no two ESOPs will be exactly alike. For example, each company may be in a different stage of development, or more likely, the corporate cultures will vary significantly.

FEDERAL AND PROVINCIAL GOVERNMENTS

Federal and provincial governments provide very few tax incentives for ESOPs. Although there is some limited provincial ESOP legislation, federally there is no legally mandated format for ESOPs. This lack of interest by the federal government has a positive side; Canadian companies are free to devise ESOPs to meet their particular needs and objectives through different legal entities without bureaucratic interference. Examples of these differences follow.

Private Company

Perhaps a private company wishes to create an ESOP based on a share purchase plan, but has no intention of going public. The plan is to offer stock options to only a handful of key employees. In addition the company is seeking to finance growth by encouraging employees to purchase company shares through the ESOP. Note that both plans will increase the number of shareholders. If the company intends to remain a private corporation, consideration must be given to the impact of the increase in shareholders in light of securities legislation. For example, shares purchased by the employees, if the shares come out of treasury stock, will mean the amount of shares held by the previous shareholders will be reduced, or "diluted." Every share taken up by the option holders will also have the dilution effect on the previous shareholders. Security legislation requires, under certain circumstances, depending upon the percentage of dilution, require the approval of previous shareholders. Also consider that should a company sell shares to more than 50 outside shareholders, it is deemed to be a public company, and therefore, must produce a prospectus. Employees are exempt from this rule; however, if the company does find itself with 50 outside shareholders, it may be a costly exercise to implement an ESOP when the full prospectus is required under security legislation.

Public Company

In another scenario, assume a public corporation offers both its key employees and all its employees a broad-based stock option program as a non-cash financial reward for outstanding performance and loyalty to the company. In this case, perhaps, the focus of the ESOP would be strengthening communication between the company and its workers for the purpose of boosting motivation and enhancing productivity by offering employees a part of the company's success. This type of incentive-oriented plan represents the most common ESOP offered by larger Canadian employers. The issuer in this kind of plan may have to meet disclosure requirements, or may be exempt. Moreover, because a company is publicly traded, the rules of the listing stock exchange must also be taken into consideration, both during the set-up and in the subsequent operation of the stock option plans.

Private Going Public

Consider now a company seeking to establish an ESOP as a first step in a complex restructuring program. One possible example is a small, private enterprise that has decided to change its corporate status by making an initial public offering. The purpose of the proposed ESOP is to provide an injection of capital to cover the cost associated with the ESOP. In addition, the company hopes to set up a plan that will be attractive to its employees so that they may benefit from the company moving from a private company to a public company. This change in status would require the corporation to address a host of legal issues in establishing the share purchase plans. One major issue to be addressed is the amount of share options or stock options that are given to employees one year prior to the IPO. Stock exchanges limit the amount of stock that can be issued during this period. Another major example would be the amount or the price paid for the shares or for the options by the employees in that period prior to the IPO. There are tremendous implications to the company and to the employees if the securities commission deems that the shares were offered at below fair market value to the employees.

Employee Buyout

The last scenario is an employee takeover of the company, one that is much less common during periods of economic growth. This scenario could be dubbed the Algoma Model after the dramatic transformation of Algoma Steel, Canada's third-largest steel producer, which saw the unions become partners in business during a downturn in the steel industry. Here, the purpose of the ESOP would be to allow the workers to reduce their employer's debt load, by swapping part of their wages for shares. In some instances, such as the Algoma Steel example, these deals are brokered by a government seeking to prevent a shakedown in a significant sector of the economy. However, this type of employee buyout raises serious issues of corporate governance, all of which must be carefully weighed and considered in advance, prior to bringing in an ESOP.

SPECIFIC LEGAL ISSUES RELATED TO AN ESOP

Right to Representation on the Board of Directors

This element is likely to be a more significant factor in situations where the ESOP is intended to effect an overhaul of the company's corporate culture, and clearly in situations like the Algoma Model there is no clear answer to whether or not employees that are part of an ESOP should have a right to representation on the board of directors. It is an issue that has split the ESOP community. In many cases the decision results from the corporate culture and the trust between the various stakeholders in the company. In a unionized company the unions usually require that representation, if they are to look at an ESOP as a means of supplementing wage concessions. However, where ESOPs are put into place not as a methodology to restrict the employees but as a means to allow them to participate in the growth of the company, there is a tendency to develop over time the right of the employees to representation on the board of directors. Studies in the United States have shown that a majority of companies do not put an employee on the board of directors in the first few years of the ESOP. However, after five or six years of operating the ESOP, corporations tend to appoint employees to the board of directors, as all stakeholders begin to understand and respect the issues that are involved in running the corporation, and trust each other to do what is best for the growth of the company.

Veto Rights

The plan should spell out whether the participating employees will have the power to veto corporate transactions and what transactions would be affected. Veto rights would be considered only when the employees have a substantial voting block of shares in the company and, therefore, a substantial say in the operation of the company. The following list is illustrative of key veto elements for consideration:

- new issues of treasury shares by the corporation,

- amalgamations and mergers with other corporations,

- sales of significant assets,

- material acquisitions,

- certain material business decisions as defined or specified in the agreement, and

- the recruitment of the company's executive officer.

Tag-Along Rights

The plan must indicate what rights the participating employees will have in the event that the principal shareholders were to agree to sell their shares in the company to a third party. The key issue is whether the employees have the right to participate in the proposed share transfer. Can they tag along and sell their shares at the same prices as the principal shareholders?

Drag-Along Rights

The plan must also indicate whether the principal shareholders have the right to require the participating employees to sell their shares to a third party for the same price as that agreed to by the principal shareholders. Most plans have drag-along rights, at a minimum, and often both drag-along and tag-along rights as well.

Confidentiality Rights

Generally speaking, employees participating in the ESOP plan will have access to financial information about the company that was previously available only to a select few shareholders. In that case, the issuing shareholder should consider including a confidentiality clause in a shareholders' agreement prior to launching the equity-based compensation plan.

Put Options

The plan should state whether or not participating employees have the right to require the employer or principal shareholder to purchase all or part of their shares, at a specified price, following a specified triggering event. An example of the triggering event would be death, disability, or termination of an employee.

Call Options

If applicable, the plan should state whether the employer or principal shareholder has the right to require the participating employees to sell all or part of their shares, at a specified price, following a specific triggering event. Again, examples would be employee death, disability, or termination.

Preemptive Rights

The plan should specify whether the existing shareholders are entitled to maintain their existing percentage ownership, following the issuance by the company of additional treasury shares. For example, if the company has to raise interim financing for an expansion phase, and does this through issuing treasury shares to a new investor, all previous shareholders will have their existing percentage ownership diluted. Some ESOPs require that shareholders maintain their existing percentage ownership even in cases of dilution.

Resale Rights

This element is of particular importance in private corporations. The ESOP must state what rights the participating employees will have to realize their profit from the ownership interest they are to acquire, whether the shares are to be sold back to the issuing employer, and whether the employer will undertake to sell the shares to other employees. This issue has important tax implications to the employee, which were discussed in Chapter 6: ESOPs and Income tax. In addition, if the employer undertakes to sell shares to other employees, a mini-market would be required within the corporation.

FINANCIAL ASSISTANCE

Under the *Canada Business Corporations Act (Canada)* (CBCA) and the *Business Corporations Act (Ontario)* (OBCA), a corporation may provide its employees with financial assistance whether through a loan, guarantee, or otherwise in order to facilitate the purchase of shares under an ESOP. Companies in other jurisdictions across Canada should check with the local legal authorities to determine their provincial regulations. However, the corporation must meet the solvency test outlined in CBCA. Essentially, there must not be any reasonable grounds for believing that the corporation is, or would be after providing the financial assistance, unable to pay its liabilities as they become due. Nor must there be any reasonable grounds for believing that the realizable value of the corporation's assets, excluding the amounts of any financial assistance provided, would be less than the aggregate of the corporation's liabilities and stated capital of all classes. This requires that a company cannot put the company or the employees in a situation whereby loaning funds for the employees to purchase shares in the company will put the company's creditors at risk, as well as the employees at risk for potentially investing in an insolvent company.

Note that in the case of a corporation incorporated under CBCA, any shares purchased by employees with the financial assistance of the issuing employer must be held by a trustee. (see "Loan Forgiveness" page 126.)

OWNERSHIP ISSUES

If the issuing employer intends to remain a private corporation, retention of control in the hands of the corporate founders is likely to be a major concern. This tends to give rise to special legal considerations such as share ownership in the event of the employee /shareholder's death, or in the event of a family breakdown. In either of these two cases, the shares assigned to or purchased by an employee could constitute a valuable asset and may become the subject of a property division claim.

At the same time, the other shareholders and the corporation itself will want to be able to control the ownership of company shares, even when faced with the division of an employee/shareholder's property.

CBCA AND OBCA

The CBCA and most other corporate statutes required that there be constraints on the sale of shares as a condition of obtaining private corporation status. Transfers of the shares of a private company require the approval of the company directors or other shareholders. The most common way of addressing this matter is by means of a detailed shareholders' agreement, which generally includes rights of first refusal or some type of buy-sell clause. Alternatively, the director's resolution can authorize the issuing of the shares and may require such conditions and rights to be inscribed on the face of each stock certificate. The other side of the coin is the possibility that a shareholder might be deemed to be in control of a private corporation for the purposes of the *Income Tax Act (Canada)* (ITA). Although most

ESOPs create the situation of having minority shareholders, it is possible that for certain classes of shares that have been issued by the company in a previous restructuring that certain employees, although part of a minority group in the ESOP, may actually have majority control of certain types of shares, which is not allowed, according to the act.

The CBCA expressly allows a corporation to repurchase issued shares in order to fulfill the terms of the agreement under which the corporation has an option to purchase shares owned by a director, officer, or employee of the corporation. The equivalent *Ontario Business Corporation Act* is even more explicit in that it specifically states to apply to former as well as current directors, officers, and employees. This means the plan must allow for liquidity of the shares either through repurchase by the corporation or in some other manner.

Under Section 25 of the OBCA, the articles of a corporation may authorize the issue of any class of share in one or more series and fix the rights, privileges, restrictions, and conditions to be attached to the shares. However, unless the articles make such a provision, holders of shares of a class or in some cases of a series, are entitled to vote separately as a class or series upon a proposal to amend the articles, or to create a new class or series of shares equal or superior to the shares of their class or series. Depending on the rights, privileges, and restrictions attached to the employee shares, a corporation might have to consider the ramifications these provisions impose on the company. Therefore, when developing an ESOP, especially in a private company, it is important to keep the plan as simple as possible. The more share classes available, the more complex communicating the issues to the employees is and the more difficult it is to create the trust necessary to make the plan successful.

PERPETUITIES AND RESTRAINT ON ALIENATION

Two legal rules that must be considered in devising the ESOP or a stock option plan for a private corporation are the rules against perpetuities and restraint on alienation. This means that the assets of the plan, being the shares owned by the employees, cannot be restricted in their transferability; however, at some point in time they do acquire the ability to be transferred and conveyed. In a landmark case, the court held that any provision in a share purchase plan designed to restrict the disposal of shares by employees, thereby offending the rule against perpetuities, or constituting a restraint on alienation, would be void.

Therefore, the plan must allow for some type of transfer at some point in time for the employees.

TRANSFERRING AND ASSIGNMENT OF SHARES

As employee shares have been issued as part of the corporate structure, the issuing company would not want these shares to be held by persons other than employees. One reason for this would be, for example, if the company has plans to do an IPO. It would be very difficult to quickly find all the shareholders if the original shareholders have transferred their shares to unknown third parties. In such cases, a condition should stipulate that the participating employee must transfer his or her shares to another employee within a specified time period following a retirement or a termination, failing which the shares would be surrendered to the corporation for cancellation upon repayment for them.

ESOP LEGAL DESIGN ISSUES

The precise structure of each proposed ESOP can be completely unique. Perhaps the most obvious distinction is between a share purchase plan and a stock option plan. ESOPs and stock options offer two very different kinds of investment vehicles, and each gives rise to a unique set of legal issues. The choice between establishing an ESOP that includes a share purchase plan or a stock option plan, or both, and the overall decision on which employees will have access to the plan, will generally also be a function of the underlying motivation for establishing the plan in the first place. If the intention is to enhance employee loyalty, enthusiasm, and productivity all the way down the production line, the choice is likely to be a broad-based plan with a share equity component. On the other hand, if the intention is to keep a lid on the cash portion of escalating executive salaries, perhaps a key-person stock option plan would form a significant part of executive remuneration. Obviously access to such plans would be restricted appropriately.

Generally, an ESOP sets time limits for a participating employee to purchase stock and/or options. The employee would be required to make periodic investments into an account over a set amount of time, and the funds would be withdrawn to purchase shares. By contrast, a stock option allows its holder to acquire the option stock at a pre-determined price at the time of the holder's choosing. For the holder of a stock option, entry into the stock is essentially risk-free, because the holder will exercise the option only when the stock price has risen above the fixed price that he or she can buy the stock for. If the stock price falls below that initial price, the holder will not exercise the option and therefore has no investment in the company.

Changing market conditions and the changing fortunes of the issuing company over time will lead to gains or losses in the value of its stock. Unlike the holder of a stock option, an employee participating in an ESOP with a share purchase plan has no control over the unit price of each stock acquisition. Investment specialists would be quick to point out a decline in the stock price for the employee even though its paper loss would have to be explained and communicated to the employees. This would tend to be counterproductive in the case of an ESOP designed to boost employee morale. As a result, the issuing company may elect to set up a matching investment scheme to boost the participating employee's overall return. Alternatively, it might establish a protection scheme such as a guaranteed share repurchase clause, a type of "put" clause that establishes the minimum value at which the shares can be sold back to the company. For example, if the employees invest in the company at $10 a share and at some point in time designated by the company, the employee could then "put" those shares back to the company, the shares are guaranteed so that no matter what the value of the company at that point in time, the employees would always get at least their $10 per share. The advantage to the employees is that they have tremendously reduced their risk in terms of their investment. The disadvantages to the company are that if the company does have a decline in value of a substantial amount they may have a liquidity problem in trying to meet the "put" clauses from various shareholders. One way around this is to put a cap on the amount of puts in any one year.

The issuing company may also provide employees with optional financial assistance in order to help them participate in the ESOP or the share option plan. In the case of outright equity ownership by means of participation in an ESOP, however, leverage purchasing increases the investor's potential risk. Again, issuing companies may be tempted to provide a "quick-fix" solution for the participating employees in the event of the downturn of the value of shares, though a mechanism like loan forgiveness.

Both sides of downside-protection schemes—guaranteed share repurchase and loan forgiveness—give rise to a number of significant legal considerations, which will be addressed in detail in the next section. Loan forgiveness, for example, is similar to a guaranteed share repurchase clause because the company basically has loaned the money to the employee to purchase shares and, in certain circumstances, does not ask for the loan to be paid back. For example, if the employee borrows $1,000 to buy shares in the company and is required to pay back that loan by the third year, the company in the third year could forgive that loan, thereby reducing the employee's risk in terms of investing in the company.

DOWNSIDE-PROTECTION SCHEMES

Any outright equity investment involves the risk of loss. Volatility of equity markets, both private and public, the inevitability of cyclical market performance, and unforeseen changes in consumer trends all add potential risk for an equity investor. ESOP participants are not immune to these risks. When an equity plan is part of an ESOP, the employees must understand that they are investing in a company that has risk. Arguably, the very nature of company-wide ESOPs increases the possibility of an investor being taken unaware by the sudden drop in the value of his shareholdings. This is because enrolment in an ESOP generally involves a standard form agreement by means of which the employee subscribes to a periodic investment program and a series of payroll deductions. Although ESOPs are intended to be long-term investments, there is rarely any investment advice sought by the employee, provided by the employer at the time of enrolment. Although ESOP companies may ensure that this investment advice is available to employees, they usually don't take advantage of that advice. The forced savings of periodic investment into an ESOP is attractive to lower-income employees, and for some, the company ESOP might well represent their only form of savings. All of these factors increase the possibility that a sudden downslide in a company's performance and a corresponding tumble in share value could convert the ESOP from a source of employee loyalty and heightened morale into employee alienation, which, is to say the least, a human resource liability. Most companies would prefer to avoid such unnecessary strains on the employee/employer relationship, and they do so by instituting a downside-protection scheme. It should be noted that payroll deductions, although popular, are not the only way for private companies to institute a stock equity plan, especially if the amounts involved are within the capabilities of employees to pay through other means.

Guaranteed Repurchase Scheme

One option is a guaranteed share repurchase right contained within the terms of the ESOP. This right functions like a "put" option in the hands of participating employees whereby they have the right to require the company to purchase their shares at a specified minimum price. (Note that this scheme could be a taxable benefit in the hands of the employee.) The employee benefits through this scheme because he or she has limited the downside risk by being able to obtain a minimum price in future if conditions warrant.

Lowering the Average Cost of Shares

Another option would be for the employer to advance a one-time "bonus" of additional shares at the current depressed prices in a quantity in proportion to each employee's previous shareholdings. This would shore up the employee's paper losses due to a deterioration in the share prices. As a result of the increased number of shares being held by the participants plan, each employee's per share cost would be averaged down. The lower average price would, in turn, allow the employees to recover their losses more quickly as the value of their shares rebounds. From the employee's perspective, the advisability of lowering the average cost of the shares would depend on the likelihood of the company regaining its share values in the future.

Loan Forgiveness

Loan forgiveness is a common downside-protection scheme in situations where the company plans to offer financial assistance to participating employees. This scheme may provide additional incentive for employees to participate in the proposed ESOP or stock option plan. Loan forgiveness is generally structured such that whenever shares decline in value, the corporation, which is either the lender or the guarantor, will forgive or repay the outstanding loan. (Note that the amount forgiven would constitute a taxable benefit to the employee because the employee has received a benefit without paying for it.) Therefore the Canada Customs and Revenue Agency deems that to be a constructive receipt of an asset, which is taxable in the employee's hands.

POTENTIAL FOR NON-EMPLOYEE SHAREHOLDER REPRISAL

In devising a downside-protection scheme, such as those outlined above, it is important to consult with existing, non-employee shareholders. If the overall package appears too generous in their eyes, it could lead to reprisals. For example, the minority shareholders could sue the company if they believe there was a deterioration in the asset base due to the loan-forgiveness arrangement.

POTENTIAL FOR EMPLOYEE REPRISAL

In the United States, dozens of lawsuits have been brought by employees against their employers, legal advisors, and trustees with respect to their participation in ESOPs. These actions have included claims of misuse of assets, broken promises (such as changing the schedule for benefit distribution), or excessive management remuneration at the expense of participating employees. Although the most vulnerable parties in an ESOP arrangement are typically any trustees appointed to look out for the best interests of the participants, management is also vulnerable to court action for perceived mishandling of company assets. The trustee is a person or company hired to oversee the administration and the policies of owning the shares by the employees. Therefore, the trustee's position is a critical one and should not be undertaken lightly.

SHAREHOLDERS' AGREEMENT

Perhaps the single most important component of any ESOP development process is the shareholders' agreement. The agreement should embody all the rights and obligations of the employees or shareholders, the employer, and its principals. The shareholder's agreement is a key element to protect employees and outline their rights and obligations to the company and the rights and obligations of the company to them. (See Appendix 6 for a sample agreement.)

ESOP HOLDING COMPANIES

The exemption for private companies from registration and prospectus requirements does not apply in connection to an ESOP holding company incorporated to hold all the shares belonging to the employees. The shareholders, although employees of the issuing corporation, cannot be employees of the holding company. In order to use a holding company for an ESOP for a private corporation with more than 50 participating employees, the issuer would need to apply to the Provincial Securities Commission for an order exempting the holding company from compliance. As noted above, the exemption order will normally be granted on request unless the commission suspects that it might be prejudicial to the public interest. The ESOP holding company is important for purposes of income tax considerations where the employee, by selling shares to the holding company, can benefit in a private corporation setting for the capital gains exemption. In addition, some companies would rather deal with one trustee representing all the employees than have individual employees directly owning shares in the company.

CONCLUSION

The legal matters involved in setting up an ESOP plan are fairly complex. This chapter is not meant to be an exhaustive overview of the legal issues involved in the design and implementation of an ESOP. It is important that legal representation be obtained by any company putting an ESOP into place.

Administration and Communication

OWNERSHIP IS A STATE OF MIND, a way of looking at something as part of oneself. The creation of an ownership mentality among all employees in a company requires a fully committed management group including all the owners and the board of directors. Without this it is very difficult to build and sustain an ownership culture. Simply installing an ESOP is no guarantee of more motivated and effective employees. Employees feel and act like owners only if the notion of ownership is constantly reinforced. While setting up an ESOP involves a complex series of rules and regulations, operating an ESOP company involves concepts that are simpler to describe but difficult to implement. Whereas setting up an ESOP requires competent and financial legal advisors, managing an ESOP needs constant effort to reinforce the idea of ownership. The result of this diligence by management is a high-performance company.

FOSTERING AN OWNERSHIP MENTALITY

Throughout the implementation stage and into the post-ESOP stage it is important that management help employees understand what ownership means in the company culture. Every employee will have a different understanding of ownership. For example, some employees may believe that if they become owners they will be the presidents of the company and able to make decisions at the presidential level. Others may perceive ownership as meaning that they can't be terminated from the company. If these understandings or perceptions are left unattended, especially if held by employee opinion leaders, they could become a negative force within the company. It is up to management to guide expectations by explaining what will and will not change in corporate policy. Managers will explain what is to be gained by each employee through ownership. This message should be kept as simple as possible. There should be a clear plan laid out for sharing information and for employee participation. The cost benefits that will accrue to each employee through participation in the plan are laid out frequently and consistently throughout the process. For example, during design of the ESOP, the employee questionnaire asks for employees' perceptions in terms of ownership of the company. A sample questionnaire is included in the Appendix. Constant feedback through the employee representation on the ESOP team creates understanding and communication of the issues of what it means to be an employee owner. The next major step of communication is the "blueprint," which the employees receive explaining in detail not only the design parameters of the ESOP but also the costs and benefits of the program to the employee, what is expected of the employee, and what is expected of the employer.

Finally, the goal of the communication process is to produce an employee information package, which will outline in plain language what the plan is about and, again, what is expected of the employees and what is expected of the employer. This process doesn't end after the employees become owners. ESOP communication is a continuous process.

COMMUNICATING OWNERSHIP

Communication is the critical ingredient that distinguishes what a company wants to do with an ESOP. Communication is often the single most important factor in achieving the goal of getting employees to act as owners. Communication starts immediately after the decision to develop an ESOP is made. The ESOP process takes about three to six months to complete. However, this is only the first step, and subscription to the ESOP is the end of that first step. The issuance of a share certificate, a stock option certificate, or a phantom plan unit certificate is an important milestone in creating ownership mentality. This should be made into a major event for the company, with the certificates printed on heavy stock and appropriately "official looking." The communication process, described in previous chapters, comprising continual communication of the ESOP, its design parameters, and feedback from the employees, has now culminated in the final event.

Other Communication Vehicles

Other communication vehicles will depend upon what current communication materials are used within the company and how the company intends to take to spread the message. Companies have used daily, monthly, or quarterly newsletters, focus groups, weekly sales and target reports, an ESOP annual employee meeting, an annual shareholder meeting, Internet or intranet communications, a communication committee controlled by employees, employee representation on the board of directors, and strategic planning groups.

PARTICIPATION

Studies in the United States over the last 25 years have repeatedly identified that an ESOP with a participation component outperforms one without a participation element. Participation means that the employees take on the responsibility of their particular job as well as the accountability that goes along with it by participating in decision-making in their sphere of influence within the organization. For example, a production line supervisor who has control over a particular product line has decision-making responsibility to produce that product in the most efficient and effective manner possible. He or she can make decisions that will affect the bottom line of the company participation in his or her own work place. In fact, the same studies have shown that ESOPs without employee participation might be worse than having no ESOP at all. Nevertheless, participation by itself does not result in significant corporate performance increases. It is only the combination of adopting ownership mentality and employee participation that yields the results sought.

How can a company best incorporate a participative element? The company must involve employees in any area of decision-making that directly impacts on their performance. Not every employee should be made a manager. On the contrary, managers must become true custodians of their human resources, but at the same time, those resources must be given the trust and respect due to them so they can become involved in the growth of the company towards its goals.

TWELVE SUCCESSFUL STRATEGIES FOR CREATING A PARTICIPATIVE ENVIRONMENT

1. It is important to initiate a participative structure through communications with all levels of employees. A bottom-up approach to installation works better than a top-down unilateral dictated policy change. For example, instead of a company indicating to employees that a quarterly meeting will be held to discuss the results of that quarter, each employee group would be allowed to decide how often they should meet to discuss what is important to them.

2. Participation is non-judgmental. This means that whether or not an employee decides to participate is an individual decision. Each employee must understand that through participation he or she is accepting the responsibility to improve the value of the company and, therefore, his or her own wealth creation. Employees should understand that it is not enough to follow the rule book; rather the rule book should be expanded, so that if there are better ways of achieving results, they should be implemented.

3. Each company has a different corporate culture and communication model. Therefore, a participation plan must be tailored to meet each company's needs. For example, in a high tech company where many of the employees are working on Internet and intranet applications, communication should probably be through that source. One ESOP client in a multi-media setting set up an Internet site just for communicating what's going on in the ESOP and to ask for feedback and suggestions to improve the ESOP. The site is updated monthly with summaries of employees' questions and sent out to all ESOP participants.

4. Decision-making must be encouraged at all levels, and difficult or positive decisions should also be rewarded and acknowledged. There must be some type of system in place to measure when a decision has been profitable and some reward for that profitability. For example, if a company unit has had turnover problems and

substantially cut its turnover due to specific decisions or actions, that unit should be awarded shares or options depending on the compensation policies of the company.

5. An active role must be taken by employees. A participating employee actively searches for, finds, and solves problems within the company to participate and increase the sales and profitability of the company.

6. Once a participative culture is implemented, communicated, and accepted by a work force, it is then a required expectation of all the employees. The longer an ESOP participative program is in place, the more the employees get involved, and the impact on the workplace can be substantial. First, employees who are not comfortable in a participative environment tend to leave the company, and people attracted to a participative entrepreneurial company apply for the positions. So the nature of the work force actually changes to one that is more participative.

7. Management must be aware that new skills may be required by employees in areas such as leadership, problem-solving, coaching, public speaking to groups, and so on. Many companies will institute training programs to improve the skill sets of their employees, not only in the area in which they are directly involved. Having employees participate in speaking groups, for example, will allow them to expand their expertise and be more confident talking about the company in various scenarios.

8. As with any HR initiative, participation must be continually renewed with innovative ideas from the employee themselves.

9. There must be a clear understanding of the role and responsibilities of middle management staff and supervisors. For example, a detailed organization chart showing the roles and responsibilities will allow each employee to assess his or her position within the corporate structure.

10. There can be no system of responsibility without a system of accountability, including measuring results and their consequences. Reward systems can take many forms; they can be based on profitability, or increased revenues, depending upon the key drivers of value within the company. Once those key value drivers are

identified, a compensation or a reward system can be put into place to reward those increases and drivers.

11. Participation means that employees must have access to the resources, such as time and mentoring, that lead to accountability.

12. Employees must become business literate within the context of their company and their interests. Many companies, once they have established an ESOP, implement open-book management policies, which increase their employees' financial understanding of how their company works, how the company can increase value, and how the employee can affect that value.

TRAINING

The goal of most ESOPs is to have each employee reach his or her maximum potential as a person and as an employee. This requires two types of training; the first involves helping employees understand the meaning and proper use of an ESOP in achieving corporate goals and what that means to employees themselves. This can be achieved through various means such as ESOP advisory teams where the employees learn the administrative aspects of ESOPs and how to communicate the benefits of ESOPs to other employees and to the community at large. The second type of training is more traditional and makes that employee the best he or she can be in his or her area of responsibility. The employees must be given the time and the budget to accomplish these goals.

For example, many companies will set up specific training budgets that are then allocated to different divisions in the corporations. Each division is responsible for deciding the type of training and how that budget is to be used.

Information Management

Important decisions require complete information. Accurate information when coupled with ownership, participation, and training, can have be very powerful force in the hands of employees. Information would include anything that relates specifically to that employee in their area of work. For example, a marketing coordinator of a company needs to have information on the unit costs of the marketing department, how efficient the marketing budget has been, and how effective sales people have been. The coordinator can impart this information to the employees and shore up any weaknesses in the company.

The key element to empowering employees in an ESOP is business literacy, which is strengthened by open-book management. Business literacy is a subset of open-book management. Once employees are taught how to read balance sheets and financial statements, they can now suggest ways to broaden the scope of the type of information that could be collected beyond solely economic information. Some companies already have a culture where financial information is freely given out to employees on a regular basis. In this type of environment, it is important to ensure that the employees are capable of interpreting these financials and understanding how they influence the key value drivers in a company. A key value driver is one that is important for the company to generate either revenues or profitability in the company. For a company that is in software marketing, a key value driver would be the ability and the length of time it takes to get a new product to market.

The nature of the information that is distributed to employees varies between companies and divisions depending on the needs and cultural openness of the company. Some employers worry that by disclosing their financial information they risk exposing sensitive internal marketing and pricing data to their competitors. Other employers give out all the information that others reserve for only key executives. The degree of disclosure is company-specific.

Nevertheless, companies with a more closed or secretive culture must begin to slowly share information to improve the financial knowledge of their employees. Employees can be given more information as they appear capable of handling it. The most successful strategy is to disclose an appropriate level of information so that each individual can assess his or her impact on the corporation. One area of financial disclosure that is sacrosanct: employee salaries. Studies have shown that 99 per cent of ESOP companies do not disclose such information nor is it demanded by the employees. On the contrary, most employees demand that it be kept confidential.

CONCLUSION

Administration and communication of the ESOP is crucial to its success. How one goes about this communication model is critical and depends upon many factors. The key factor to effective communication is the openness of management and owners in allowing employees to be fully informed and trained on how to use financial information within the company. For many companies this is difficult at first. Eventually, though, ESOPs tend to make it easier to create an open-book management culture. It is important for the stakeholders in the company to understand that an ESOP is an organic process and administration and communication of the ESOP means it is a continual process.

Once the ESOP is in place and the employees have subscribed for the shares or for the stock options, the work of the ESOP is just beginning. This chapter on administration and communication has begun the examination of post-ESOP issues. The remaining chapters will explain the additional measures that must be undertaken so that the ESOP can achieve its original goals and objectives.

Post-ESOP Issues

PROFIT-SHARING AND OPEN-BOOK MANAGEMENT

An ESOP is a long-term incentive plan through which wealth is created over several years. During a short-term time frame, however, many employees prefer a more immediate monetary reward. Profit-sharing can be used as a short-term reward system complementary to the ESOP. Profit sharing works with the ESOP to motivate employees to participate in the ongoing wealth creation of the company.

In this chapter we will discuss the types of profit-sharing plans and how profit-sharing can be utilized in conjunction with an ESOP to achieve corporate objectives.

DEFINITION AND TYPES OF PROFIT-SHARING PLANS

Profit-sharing is a compensation program that makes payments to employees over and above their base salaries or wages. These additional payments are determined by the level of the corporation's profits. For example, Valley City Manufacturing Company of Dundas, Ontario, a small manufacturer of architectural woodwork and cabinetry, has a classic combination profit-sharing plan. The company distributes 27 per cent of before-tax profits among the employees, prorated to their base salary.

In Canada, there are four major types of profit sharing plans:

- Cash

- Deferred profit-sharing plan (DPSP)

- Employees' profit-sharing plans (EPSP)

- Combination plans

Cash

All payments are made to the employees in cash which is treated as income, and is fully taxable. The payments are deductible for the employer, and there is no limit on the amount of the deduction. However, the income tax must be withheld at source. Cash plans are the most common type of profit-sharing plans in Canada.

Deferred Profit-Sharing Plans (DPSP)

DPSPs are established under the authority of the Canada *Income Tax Act*. The employer makes contributions to a trust fund on behalf of employees up to a certain maximum, similar to employees contributing to a self-directed RRSP. The act limits in two ways the amounts that can be contributed:

- the total contribution made by an employer and an employee to DPSPs, registered pension plans (RPPs), and Registered Retirement Savings Plans (RRSPs); and

- the total contributions made by the employer to a DPSP.

For a DPSP, the employer would set up a trust fund at a financial institution. Within the limits set out by the act, all contributions are deductible expenses for the employer. Taxes on the earnings and capital gains of the trust are deferred until they are withdrawn, just as for RRSPs. Although there are some restrictions, the fund can be invested in most types of Canadian securities.

Employee Profit-Sharing Plans (EPSP)

Similar to DPSPs, EPSPs have a legal basis through the *Income Tax Act*, and in EPSPs the funds are placed in a trust by the employer on behalf of the employee. However, unlike DPSPs, income tax on EPSPs must be withheld by the employer. Another difference is that there are no limits on the types of investments, and the earnings and capital gains of the trust are taxed each year. EPSPs are very rare due to these restrictions, with less than 5 per cent of all profit-sharing plans using EPSPs.

Combination Plans

A company can set up a profit-sharing plan that combines any two, or all three of the above options. For example, in a plan that is part DPSP and part cash, the company would pay the maximum allowable under the *Income tax Act* to the DPSP and pay any amount left over from the employer allocation in cash. Another possibility would be to pay half of the company's contribution to the DPSP and half in cash. The major features of any combination plan will depend on the exact proportions of the major components.

CONDITIONS REQUIRED BEFORE STARTING

When designing a profit-sharing plan, it is very important that the company's senior executives or owners ensure that the following are in place:

- Reasonable employee relations. Do the employees trust the executive team to put a profit-sharing plan into place that will benefit the employees?

- Base salaries that are at least externally competitive and internally fair.

- A high probability that there will be some profits to share. To the extent possible, this should also be true of the next year or two, which is why a profit-sharing plan is a good partner to an ESOP. Profit-sharing plans give immediate compensation to employees for achieving targeted goals and in years where there may be no profits, due to expansion or for other reasons, the ESOP will continue to have value to the employees.

- There should be some stability in the company since introducing a profit-sharing plan is itself a form of change.

- There should be good communications between management and employees on a regular basis using dependable channels of communication.

- Management must have a commitment to operate the plan but also to be prepared to deal with employees who want to be involved.

STRATEGIC ISSUES FOR MANAGEMENT

There are several issues that should be discussed prior to creating the plan or talking with the employees:

- objectives of the plan,

- type of plan,

- employee involvement, and

- employer contribution.

Objectives of the Plan

Management must have a clear idea of what it wants to achieve with a profit-sharing plan. Although plans can perform a variety of different functions, the choice of plan objectives will influence every design decision made later on.

For example, a private company that wants to attract high-quality employees may have to make the waiting period to join the plan very brief or eliminate it entirely. Profit-sharing plan objectives should be coordinated with the objectives of the ESOP, so both meet the company's goals.

Type of Plan

Many employers know the type of plan they want before they start the design process. Others believe that profit-sharing is a good concept but have not determined the specific type of plan they would like. Those employers are well advised to seek their employees' input. However, experience indicates that virtually all employees prefer a cash plan if given a choice. Therefore, for employers who know they want something other than a cash plan, that decision should be communicated.

Employer Contribution

Before establishing an employee committee, the size and definition of the company's profit-sharing contribution must be decided. Other issues to address are definition of profits, the proportion that will be available for distribution to the employees, the type of formula used to determine the employer contribution, and the timing and frequency of the payments.

Profits can be defined as either net profits before or after tax. Most companies use net profits before tax, because it is easier to calculate the amount of profits that are available for distribution on a before-tax basis. Should the plan include extraordinary gains or losses? Examples would be the sale of a building or investment gains or losses. Before making this decision an employer should determine whether the employees have significant influence on the activities in questions and, if so, include them in the process. However, if they do not have much influence, exclude them. Some companies, such as Algoma Steel, use operating profit as a basis for their calculation. Operating profit is profit that is calculated before extraordinary items and before overhead items such as interest and foreign exchange gains and losses.

A plan can use either "discretionary" or "specified" formula. Discretionary means the employer decides each year what proportion of profits will go into the plan, while specified means that the percentage of profits contributed by the company is declared at the outset of the plan. A discretionary formula should generally not be used for a broad-based employee profit-sharing plan because the company is trying to build a trust relationship with the employees. Employees understand that if they meet certain target levels there will be an amount of profit distribution based on a formula. The formula can be a straight percentage of all profits, such as 10 per cent of net profit before taxes. Alternatively, it can be a specified percentage above a certain minimum level of profit. For example, it could be 15 per cent of net profit over $200,000 after taxes. A formula can also be graduated so that the percentage of profits to be paid out increases at various points. It could provide for 10 per cent of the first $1 million; 15 per cent of the next million, and 20 per cent of any profits over $2 million.

The final decision is actual percentage used. The most common are 8–10 per cent or 15 per cent of the net profit before taxes.

Although these percentages are used as a general rule of thumb in the industry, employers should consider their own requirements for capital and cash flow. Alternatively, the employer contribution can be a percentage of the cash payroll. A rule of thumb is that any payment to employees should be at least 3–5 per cent of their base pay, otherwise they won't notice. However, this is a very rough guideline; employees just starting their profit-sharing plan, and who are not sure about what percentage of profits to contribute, should start low. The percentage can always be increased later, but it is very difficult to decrease the level of contribution if the company's unable to sustain the plan.

Employee Involvement

One of the most critical decisions to make at this stage is the extent to which employees will be involved in the process of designing the profit-sharing plan. Some employers sit down alone or with a couple of trusted advisors, design the plan, and then announce it, expecting the employees to be both surprised and grateful. Frequently, however, they are shocked to find that employees are surprised but also very suspicious and even hostile. In these circumstances, employees will question every design decision made. The only way to counter this is to get the employees involved in the process. This is the same process advocated for the ESOP—and for the same reasons. An employer must build up a level of trust with the employees. Having put an ESOP into place with the participatory process described earlier in this book, it would be foolish for the management group to try to implement a profit-sharing plan without taking employees' concerns into account. Therefore, by far the best way to carry out the planning is to form a committee comprising a representative cross-section of employees.

When forming the committee, choose employees who are viewed as opinion leaders by the group they represent, able to understand the concepts involved, and willing and articulate enough to act as spokespeople for their group. It is preferable that the employer select the committee members so as to obtain the characteristics mentioned above. If an ongoing committee to help administer the plan is required, employees could be elected to that.

MAJOR DESIGN ISSUES

The owner can decide these questions, or these questions can be decided by the employees involved in the design process. There are two major design issues; one is membership and allocation.

Membership

The question of "who will be in the profit-sharing plan?" must be answered for all types of plans, whether they are cash or deferred.

There are generally five ways to define membership:

- category of employment,

- length of service,

- employees who leave the company,

- union status, and

- employees who are already in an incentive plan.

The first two topics, category of employment (full-time, part-time, occasional, temporary, or contract employees) and length of service, are interconnected. All plans include full-time employees subject to a length-of-service requirement, but not all companies include part-time employees. The inclusion of contract employees has become more of an issue in recent years because many more companies are using them. If the ESOP plan includes contract employees, a parallel issue for the profit-sharing plan should also include contract employees. However, some companies feel that contract employees should not be part of the plans because only people who have committed to the company full-time should benefit from these programs.

The third membership issue concerns those employees who leave the company. These are former employees due to death, disability, retirement, or termination, or simply absent during the fiscal year, for example, due to maternity leave. The most common approach is to include them in the plan for the portion of the year that they were employed.

The company will have to decide whether or not to include any unionized employees in the profit-sharing plan. It is generally recommended that they be included as members of the plan unless there is some reason to not do so. Profit-sharing plans are, by definition, broad-based and therefore should be all-inclusive. On the other hand, there are two major reasons for exclusion of unionized employees. One is that the unionized employees often already have some sort of group incentive. The other is that union leadership is philosophically opposed to the idea of profit-sharing because officially, organized labour is opposed to profit sharing or any other form of "variable" compensation, of which ESOPs are a prime example. Depending on the union it may be very negative towards the plan, or very positive.

The final membership criterion is whether or not to include employees who are already involved in some sort of incentive plan. These could be union or non-union employees in a productivity gain sharing plan. Of the latter, the most common group are sales representatives on commission. There are two points of view about this issue. One is that such employees are already included in a "bonus" plan and including them in profit-sharing would be rewarding them twice for the same effort. The other view is that profit-sharing is all-inclusive, meaning everybody should be in the plan; commissions or similar payments are really just part of the employee's regular earnings.

When establishing membership criteria for the profit-sharing plan, the membership requirements for the ESOP that already exists should be examined so that the two plans compensate the appropriate groups.

Allocation

Allocation is simply a decision on how to divide the funds among the members of the plan. There are six major factors to be discussed:

- earnings,

- job levels,

- attendance,

- length of service,

- merit ratings, and

- contributions by the employee.

To use earnings the employer contribution is divided into the total cash earnings of the members of the plan; the technical term is "prorated to earnings." Using earnings means that an employee's share of the profits is roughly comparable to his or her contribution in creating them, assuming a reasonably equitable salary administration program. If not, job levels can be used to determine contributions. All jobs are grouped into categories such as executives, all other management, and non-management, with contribution formulas determined by the company.

A portion of the fund is allocated to each group and then divided within the group using some other criteria. These criteria could be based on achievement of group targets in the areas of sales or cost reduction, employee turnover, divided equally, or prorated to the earnings within each group.

Attendance can be used for allocation to improve or maintain attendance levels. Points are given for each hour worked, and the fund is allocated to each individual in proportion to the number of points held. Points should be given for vacation time to avoid discriminating against employees with longer service who usually get more vacation.

Length of service or seniority is very common in allocation formulas; especially to reduce turnover. Points can be given for each year of service, usually counted as of the last day of the fiscal period for which profits are calculated. Most companies do place a maximum on the number of years that can be recognized believing that most employees do not continually increase their contribution to profitability beyond a certain point.

Merit ratings are evaluations of the performance of the employee by one or more levels of supervision. These ratings can also be used to decide allocations. For this system to work, an effective performance management system is essential. Since many companies do not have a system, and one can be difficult to develop, merit ratings should be avoided in the allocation formula. Merit systems reward individual performance, whereas profit-sharing encourages and rewards group behaviour. It is counterproductive to encourage the opposite.

Some profit-sharing plans are established to encourage employee savings and/or investments. Such plans often try to reward employees for their own contribution to a fund by partially or wholly matching the employee's contribution. For example, if the employee contributes a dollar the employer may allocate 50 cents to the fund.

The final option is to use combinations of these factors. Combinations are appropriate where there are multiple objectives for the plan or for companies that want to reflect different employee demographics.

Choosing an Allocation Formula

There are three major objectives when selecting an allocation formula. First, the formula should reinforce the objectives set for the plan. If, for example, the objective was to encourage employees to stay with the company, length of service should be used in the formula. Or to ensure that the payout is proportionate to the employee's contribution to profitability, either earnings or job level are used. Second, the formula should reflect the values of the employees. The best way to ensure this is to use an employee committee to help develop the formula. Finally, try to keep the formula as simple as possible while fulfilling the first two criteria. Simplicity is a major virtue in designing both profit- sharing plans and ESOPs.

Conclusion

A profit-sharing plan should be seen as a complementary employee incentive, not an equivalent for the incentives generated by the ESOP. Profit-sharing plans include many of the same issues as the ESOP, in process and design elements. An effective profit-sharing plan will satisfy employees in the short term while the ESOP will keep the employees content in the long term.

OPEN-BOOK MANAGEMENT

Open-book management (OBM) programs are useful both for ESOPs and for profit-sharing so that employees can understand the plans and be motivated by the benefits.

OBM can get everyone in the company "up to speed" to build a better business, one that works well and increases in value. OBM involves clear, relevant, and open communication throughout a company, to create the link between what an employee does day to day and the objectives of the company as a whole. In order for OBM to succeed, top management must be engaged and onside first. If owners and management are reluctant to share financial information with their employees, an open-book management policy is difficult to implement. However, financial information is readily available through several sources, including the Internet. We can usually determine a competitor's salaries by simply asking people who work there. Overhead is a little trickier but can be extrapolated by elimination of information. Certainly, there are risks in disclosing financial information. The question is whether management wants to exchange those risks for the benefits of OBM. By adopting OBM, the company can develop something their competitors may not be able to match, a highly motivated, knowledgeable work force within the entire company, working towards the same goals.

However, it is important that the ESOP be implemented first, so that the employees become owners of the company, and are eager to implement an OBM policy to learn more about the company, achieve results, and contribute to the increase in the value of the company. Because OBM answers all their questions, employees tend to be very receptive to this type of program. OBM can be applied in small private businesses or in large public companies. It applies to unionized and non-unionized businesses alike, and across the full range of industries.

Proper implementation of an OBM program starts with identifying employees' needs in terms of meeting corporate targets. Without a target and a plan for how employees can affect value, it is impossible for them to evaluate their own performance.

In conclusion then, OBM is a concept that must be driven from the top down. OBM is not to be delegated; it is a process of continual learning, a sharing process, a long-term commitment by the employees to the business and to their fellow employees, an attitude of management, and a change in culture. OBM doesn't replace strong leading management but enhances it.

TRANSITION ISSUES

An ESOP is organic; it will grow and change to meet the changing needs of the company, its culture, and its employees. These changes may come quickly or slowly— but they will come. Once the ESOP has been put into place transition issues will arise. These issues are

- expansion of the company,

- contraction of the company,

- dilution,

- change in nature of the work force,

- liquidity event,

- repurchase liability, and

- apathy.

Expansion of the Company

Whether it is a high tech company growing at 25 to 50 per cent per annum or a more traditional company growing at 5 to 15 per cent per annum, growth brings its own issues for the ESOP plan. Although the plan will have projected growth rates for at least the first three years of the plan, the company may grow faster than assumed. Therefore the allocation of the shares or the options may have been taken up sooner than expected. This creates a demand by the employees for more ownership percentage above and beyond that initially anticipated by the original ownership group. How the ownership group responds to the demand for more shares issues will determine how the ESOP will grow from that point onwards.

Various industry studies show that the percentages given to employee groups have grown substantially over the last several years, starting out in the range of 10 to 20 per cent and moving up as high as 30 to 40 per cent in some instances. Depending on the company, the original ownership group may not wish to increase the percentage ownership among the ESOP, due to a number of factors. First, as the value of the company grows, giving up a bigger percentage of the company means a large amount of money given up by the original ownership group. Second, as the company is expanded it will need additional capital. It may need to obtain interim financing or raise additional capital, therefore diluting the current owners' percentage. The ownership group may be very concerned that it could potentially lose control of the company by giving up too much ownership percentage to the employees at this point in time. There is however, usually a compromise level that will satisfy both the employees and the ownership group. Otherwise, eventually, the ownership group will have to decide whether it wants to dilute its percentage ownership to the point of losing control. The key to having a winning compromise is to be conservative with the initial share allocations, increase them on an annual basis, and communicate the reasons for the share allocations and why the percentages that were chosen are correct for the company going forward. It is not so much the quantity of the shares that are owned by the employees that matters, but that the shares or options are given out on a fair basis, and that the plan must take into account the contributions of the key management team and compensate them accordingly. Failure to address these issues as the plan grows can cause problems among the key management group, eventually having a negative influence on the growth and value of the company.

Contraction of the Company

A contraction can occur from either internal causes, such as a market, product, or service that was no longer competitive, internal disputes, and lawsuits, or external causes such as economic or industry-wide downturns. US studies have shown that most companies with ESOPs do better at protecting themselves in a contraction than non-ESOP companies. Contractions can be very stressful times for employees who sense that sales and profitability are down, may be worried about their jobs and the future of the company. ESOPs can be used to advantage in a contraction, if the proper foundations have been laid and communication is effective.

One large engineering company in Canada found itself in a major downturn and was facing bankruptcy proceedings. The company was 100 per cent ESOP-owned, and the employees decided that they were going to make this company successful through wage rollbacks and tightened their belts to get the company through the recession. Two years later, the company was back on track. Three years on, the company completed a public offering in which many employees realized gains of hundreds of thousands of dollars on their investment. A senior vice president of this company we interviewed stated that she believed the only reason that the company was able to get through the recession and avoid bankruptcy was that the company was employee-owned.

An ESOP-owned trucking company knew it was going into a severe downturn and had to lay off about 30 per cent of the work force. Company management, having set up a proper ESOP plan with open communication, took the problem to the employees. It was the employees themselves who decided who would be laid off. The company was able to survive the recession, come back stronger than ever, and within two years hire back 90 per cent of the people it had laid off.

Using an ESOP successfully means communicating the company's problems in an open and forthright manner. The employees are now stakeholders in the company; decisions that are taken for the benefit of the company, even difficult decisions, will be taken in the spirit of cooperation.

Dilution

Dilution occurs when the company needs to attract external investment and has to sell a portion of its treasury stock. Dilution also occurs when stock options are given out to either employees or third parties for services rendered. Dilution means that a current shareholder who owns 5 per cent of a company for example may be diluted down to 3 per cent if additional treasury shares are issued from the company. Again, dilution is not necessarily a good or a bad thing— it is a fact of life. The company must explain why dilution is taking place, what the company hopes to achieve by diluting the shareholdings, and obtain the understanding of the employees for the necessity of the dilution.

Change in Nature of the Work Force

Once an ESOP has been in place for several years, many ESOP companies experience a change in their work force. Inevitably, a certain percentage of employees are not comfortable with an entrepreneurial environment. This can range from 5 to 10 per cent of the work force that decline to participate in any kind of share scheme or stock option plan. These people are risk-averse and virtually nothing can induce them to participate. Over time, a portion of these people, seeing the results of the ESOP, may decide to participate and become part of the plan, due generally to peer pressure. However, a certain percentage will never be comfortable in an ESOP company. These people tend to drift away from the company, and people who are entrepreneurial in spirit and want to be part of an ESOP company are attracted to the company. So the general nature of the ESOP actually strengthens over time. Although this is a transition for the company, it should be regarded as a positive growth of the ESOP culture within that company.

Liquidity Event

The number-one question asked by employees considering joining an employee share plan is how are they going to get their money out. The liquidity event is the key event that will allow the employees to liquidate their investment and see a return on their assets. Because ESOPs are a long-term incentive plan, this may involve planning over a 5-, 10- or even a 15-year time frame. Examples of liquidity events are companies going public, a third-party buyout of either all or a portion of the company, an acquisition or merger with another company, and an employee buyout of the company. The liquidity event is unique to each company. In the high-tech community many employees look forward to an IPO as their liquidity event. However, IPOs are dependent upon market forces, which most companies cannot control; it is more likely that a company that has been properly managed and is growing will receive an offer at some point by a third party. At this point, the company has to be prepared to decide whether it is ready to sell.

The employees must be constantly apprised of any potential liquidity events that are planned for the future. However, a liquidity event may never occur.

Repurchase Liability

The repurchase liability can have a dramatic impact on the cash flow of a company. A repurchase liability is a liability of the company to purchase back the shares that employees own when they leave the company through death, disability, or termination. Generally, the repurchase price and the terms of that payment are stated in the shareholders' agreement. The company must review the demographics of its work force and be aware that there will be a time when it will have to start repurchasing shares from its employees. There are various mechanisms to account for this repurchase liability. Some companies will plan a liquidity event to fund the repurchase liability. Others will look at setting up a sinking fund so that they can retire a certain portion of shares each year and plan for that retirement.

Apathy

The major issue that the ESOP can present for both the employees and for senior management is apathy: the longer the ESOP has been in place, the more it is taken for granted. Although this is human nature, it is important that the excitement and the original intent of the ESOP be perpetually renewed through various means and mechanisms. For example, shareholder meetings can be made into an event where shareholders are treated to a banquet, party, or awards ceremony that allows them to celebrate the company's achievements. Changes to the ESOP can be made periodically to keep it current. These must be communicated through a two-way process; it is only with continual effort from employees and employers that the original reasons for and objectives of the ESOP remain valid. If these objectives have changed, the

ESOP may have to be modified and re-energized. If the ESOP is no longer achieving its objectives, or if the employees feel they have achieved their goals through the ESOP, it may be time to liquidate the ESOP and look for other means of motivation for the employees.

CONCLUSION

As the ESOP grows and matures with the company, more sophisticated design issues may occur. For example, the acquisition or startup of foreign companies will mean hiring employees in those countries and bringing them into the scope of the original ESOP plan. Cross-border ESOPs are very much a current topic, as even the smallest companies have representation and employees in various countries.

The next chapter will talk about international ESOPs.

CHAPTER TEN

International ESOPs

MANY CANADIAN COMPANIES FIND that to grow and prosper they have to export their goods and services, mainly to the United States. In the high tech field as much as 90 per cent of sales can go to other parts of the world. This has led many private companies, both large and small, to establish offices in the United States, Europe, and Asia to take advantage of the sales opportunities in other pazrts of the world.

When a company sets up facilities in other countries, it is important to create a compensation scheme that is attractive to the local employee base so that the company grows and prospers for all of its employees. An ESOP can present an equitable plan for all employees of multinational companies by attuning employees throughout the world to the goals of the parent company. By achieving the company's goals the cross-border ESOP can increase value to an even greater extent for all the employees involved. One example of a successful cross-border ESOP is Cisco Systems, which has ESOPs in well over 20 countries.

SPECIAL ESOP ISSUES

- Legal, accounting, and tax issues vary significantly from country to country. The culture of a company can have a big impact on the nature of the plan that is put into place. Americans are more likely to look favorably at an opportunity to buy into a company than Canadians, who tend to be more conservative investors. People in the United Kingdom, because they are more familiar with ESOPs due to their longer history there, tend to be somewhere between the conservative nature of Canadians and the more aggressive nature of Americans.

- Long distance communication of the nature of the plan is an issue to be dealt with, especially when most of the work force is in Canada; the satellite businesses may not have the full impact of the communication that exists in the company's home market.

- Finding competent and experienced practitioners who can implement cross-border ESOPs is not easy. The designer must be able, through either internal capacity or external connections, to service the client in a cost-effective manner. The cost of a cross-border ESOP will generally exceed that of a domestic plan because of the complexities involved.

- The ownership group's tax position can play a role in the final structure of a cross-border ESOP. For example, if the ownership group has holding companies through which the shares in the offshore companies are held, the tax structure of the holding companies must be considered when designing the overall plan for a cross-border ESOP. Therefore, it is crucial that the structure in Canada be put in place before the cross-border ESOP, to prevent tax structural problems for the ownership group.

- Language questions, even with the Americans and British, can create difficulties because the terminologies used in certain forms may differ and will have to be researched and understood thoroughly.

- Administration for a cross-border plan is more complex and may require a more costly structure to be efficient.

APPROACHES TO CROSS-BORDER ESOPS

There are several approaches to setting up a cross-border ESOP, each with advantages and disadvantages.

Home-Country Focus

Canadian content should be the basis for the cross-border plan. The cross-border component will fall into place as a translation of the Canadian content.

Setting up a home-focussed country plan is cost effective. The plan benefits the majority of employees and can be maintained at a reasonable administrative charge on an ongoing basis. The disadvantage of such a plan is that the tax implications to the non-Canadian employees may be substantial. For example, Americans residing in the United States who own stock options in Canadian companies will have to pay higher taxes than their Canadian counterparts due to the income tax laws in the United States. Although the gains realized by those non-Canadian employees may still be substantial, they will not be as great as with a country-specific plan.

Country-Specific Plans

A second option is to create separate plans in each country to take into account the tax laws of each country and capture the indigenous benefits that exist for ESOPs. For example, one Canadian company that has subsidiaries in Spain and the United States has a plan that takes advantage of the tax laws in each country. However, even though the plans are country specific, they were coordinated to be as close as possible to the Canadian plan so that there was no advantage or disadvantage for each employee.

To take a country-specific plan and set up separate plans results in increased costs for both the administration and ongoing maintenance. The advantage that may offset these costs is that each employee will maximize the after-tax return on his or her investment. A second benefit is that the employees realize that these plans are specifically designed for them.

Offshore Trust

It may be advantageous to set up an offshore trust to hold the shares of the company, in which case there are no concerns about multiple tax jurisdictions, only the jurisdiction of the offshore country.

An offshore trust means not having to worry about the specific tax laws of each country. The administration is fairly straightforward; however, there is a large up-front fee for creating an offshore trust, and some of the tax issues are fairly complicated, increasing the maintenance costs on a ongoing basis. Also, if a company will be raising interim financing eventually, it is much more difficult to invest in an offshore company than in a company registered in the United States, the United Kingdom, or Canada. The reason is that if the deal goes sour it is much more difficult for the investor to reclaim its investment in an offshore jurisdiction.

Plan Suitability

Home-country-focussed plans should be used by companies where a vast majority, 90 per cent or more, of the employees are situated in that company. An exception to this position would be if the location of the vast majority of employees changes quickly from one country to another; in that case the plan may require a separate plan to be established in the second or third country. If a company has a majority of its employees in one country but has subsidiaries that are clearly business entities unto themselves, it may be in the interest of that company to set up separate plans by country: the benefits to be derived from having a global employee mentality may not exist. If a company is in more than three countries and of a sufficient size, it should look at the offshore trust, which will allow a more efficient utilization of a global ESOP as well as minimization of tax issues for all employees.

The preferred method for most companies is to set up a plan that meets the needs of the majority of employees. The plan can be adapted at later stages and adjusted if circumstances change.

Conclusion

As the global economy expands and more countries are able to compete in the world market, long-range planning should include an international ESOP. Although an ESOP may not be designed for several years, management should plan by communicating and educating its work force and by strategizing for that eventual day.

Understanding some of the concepts of employee ownership in Canada, the United States, and the United Kingdom will assist in developing a plan for a cross-border ESOP. The US is a major trading partner for Canada, and it has more than 25 years experience with ESOPs. The UK has been utilizing ESOPs for the last 10 years, and is regarded by many Canadian companies as an entry into the European market.

It is beyond the scope of this book to discuss the ESOPs being proposed in Asia, South America, and Europe.

EMPLOYEE OWNERSHIP IN CANADA

The use of share equity or share options as part of a compensation strategy is a relatively new phenomenon in Canada. While the design and implementation of ESOPs started during World War II (mainly in Canadian subsidiaries of American parent companies such as Sears) ESOPs did not become a serious consideration until the early 1990s. Due to lack of statistical information in Canada it is very difficult to quantify how many early adopters there were in the 1940s versus how many there are now. There is a growing awareness of ESOPs; however, Canada lags behind the United States and the European Economic Community in their use. The low rate of acceptance in Canada can be linked to government involvement, or lack thereof. Canadian ESOPs are non-legislated plans built around current tax laws or legislated plans which are governed at the provincial level. Federal legislation would likely result in a situation similar to that in the United States where studies have shown that 80 per cent of ESOPs were put into place because of the tax advantages.

The first ESOP bill in Canada was passed by Quebec in 1979, as a means to create capital pools to finance Quebec businesses by providing tax relief to Quebec investors. It took almost 10 years for other provinces to follow suit. The Ontario *Employee Ownership Plan Act* appeared in 1988. Most of Canada's provinces have some form of ESOP legislation in place today. British Columbia, whose legislation was enacted in 1989, leads the field in terms of implementation.

ESOP Legislation

Government	Legislation	Incentive
Federal	*Income Tax Act*	• RRSP eligibility for employees • Employees receive 20% matching tax credit • Available only in Saskatchewan and BC
Nova Scotia	*Share Ownership Plan Act*	• Employees receive provincial tax credit of 20%
Quebec	*Quebec Stock Savings Plan & Sociétés de Placements dans L'Entreprise Québecoise*	• 125% to 175% deduction on funds invested to a maximum of 30 per cent of employee's net income • RRSP eligible
Ontario	*Community Small Business Investment Funds Act*	• Employees receive provincial tax credit of 20 per cent on first $3,500, 30 per cent up to $15,000; a $150,000 lifetime limit
Saskatchewan	*Labour Sponsored Venture Capital Corporations Act*	• Employees receive provincial tax credit of 20 per cent • Matching Federal Tax Credit of 20% • Maximum $1,000
British Columbia	*Employee Investment Act*	• Employees receive tax credit of 20 per cent • Matching Federal Tax Credit of 20% • Maximum $1,000
Manitoba	*Manitoba Employee Ownership Fund Corporation*	• Provincial tax credit $700 • Matching federal tax credit of 20

The Evolution of ESOPs in Canada

Over the last 20 years, a number of public companies have rewarded key employees for their efforts through matching share purchase programs and in some cases, expanded the option to include all employees. The performance of such ESOP companies has been tracked by the Toronto Stock Exchange (TSE). The results build an impressive case for ESOPs, indicating increased profitability and performance.

In the mid 1990s ESOPs initiated to meet financial crises, mainly to save jobs, used provincial legislation to make the deal. These types of ESOPs have tended to be union-oriented; high-profile examples including Algoma Steel, Spruce Falls, and Canadian Airlines. Studies in the United States have shown that 90 per cent of ESOP companies near bankruptcy have turned around, which is a much higher rate than that of non-ESOP companies.

In the past five years, there has been increasing interest in both legislated and non-legislated ESOPs in private companies. A non-legislated ESOP is one that utilizes the current tax laws and is not required to comply under any specific form of federal or provincial legislation. A legislated ESOP is one that meets the requirements of specific ESOP legislation and therefore is eligible to obtain the tax-credit benefits. Legislated ESOPs exist only in certain provinces.

ESOPs are initiated by employers and employees to meet a variety of current business needs, in particular the recruiting and retention of workers in knowledge-based industries. It is estimated that between 250 and 500 Canadian companies have started such ESOPs since 1995. Non-legislated ESOPs are, in effect, compensation plans based on current tax, legal, and accounting standards. Legislated plans meet the specific legal requirements set out by their respective provinces.

A number of professional associations have lobbied the federal government to make changes to tax laws in order to encourage companies to make greater use of ESOPs. ESOP Association (Canada) (ESOPAC), the Information Technology Association of Canada (ITAC), the Canadian Advanced Technology Association (CATA), the Employee Ownership and Incentives Association (EOIA) in British Columbia, and the Alliance of Manufacturers and Exporters of Canada (AMEC), have called for a more progressive tax treatment of stock options to plug the brain drain of highly skilled Canadians.

There have been some federal tax changes initiated by the federal government, mainly in the area of stock options for public companies.

Unfortunately, there have been no significant changes to encourage ESOPs in this country. Meanwhile, Canadian high tech workers and recent graduates are packing up their diplomas and heading south to a more lucrative environment. Of course many low tech and old economy companies have to rely on very highly skilled people in key positions. They too are having trouble finding and keeping these key people, yet the government still does not acknowledge this as a problem in this country.

Conclusion

Canada lags severely behind all its major western trading partners in the area of ESOPs. In the United States 20 per cent of employees are shareowners. The UK and the European Common Market have looked at ESOPs as a means of moving into the 21st century, while Canada is stuck in the 19th century. However, because there is no specific legislation, Canadians can be very creative in putting together plans that utilize many of the benefits under the *Income Tax Act* as it now stands. There is no question, however, that the future growth of ESOPs in Canada, as in the US, depends mainly upon the articulation of good ESOP-specific legislation at the federal level.

EMPLOYEE OWNERSHIP IN THE UNITED STATES

Employee ownership in the United States generally comes in two forms. One is the ESOP familiar to Canadians, but that in the US must meet certain requirements under the tax laws. The other form is generally referred to as equity compensation plans and includes stock options and stock purchase plans.

An ESOP in the United States is a qualified, defined contribution and employee benefit plan with two special characteristics; first, it is designed to invest primarily in the stock of the employer; and second, it can use borrowed funds to acquire employer stock.

ESOPs in the United States

In the United States there were various experiments in employee ownership. For example the Sears, Roebuck and Company pension plan invested in Sears stock and became famous for making millionaires of some hourly paid manual workers. However, the laws of the United States did not recognize the concept of employee ownership until the

Revenue Act in 1921 gave tax-exempt status to stock bonus plans but on an ambiguous basis since no definition was provided. Internal Revenue Service (IRS) gave sporadic private rulings on such plans after that and added the definition of a stock bonus plan in 1943. At that time, the IRS adopted a regulation that stated benefits under a stock bonus plan were required to be distributed in the form of employer stock.

There was very little employee ownership until the 1950s when a San Francisco lawyer and investment banker named Louis Kelso started writing about employee ownership in a new way. Kelso's first book, *The Capitalist Manifesto* (Louis O. Kelso and Mortimer Jerome Adler, *The Capitalist Manifesto*, New York: Random House, 1958), written with philosopher Mortimer Adler, pointed out that for capitalism to have meaning as a workable economic system, it must have meaning to the average worker; capital ownership was too concentrated among a small group of people since just 10 per cent of US citizens owned 90 per cent of the corporate stock in the country. Kelso believed that unless more people owned significant amounts of capital, the US would have economic and social problems that would be difficult to solve. Kelso was aware that wealthy individuals often acquired capital by borrowing money. Since most banks would not be willing to lend money to a group of employees to acquire stock in their companies, Kelso's solution was for the company to borrow the money to acquire the stock for the employees.

The first leveraged ESOP, that is, financed with borrowed funds, was for the *Peninsula Newspapers* in 1956. In this and subsequent transactions, Kelso relied upon special rulings from the IRS to gain authority for the use of borrowed money to acquire employer securities for stock bonus plans. By using tax-deductible contributions to repay the debt, Kelso was able to make both principal and interest payments on these loans tax-deductible, significantly reducing the risk of financing employee buyouts. Although Kelso was successful in establishing ESOPs in a number of small companies in the 1960s, ESOPs did not receive prominent national attention until Senator Russell B. Long launched a campaign promoting support of ESOP legislation in the mid-1970s. Beginning in 1974, with the *Employment Retirement Income Security Act* (ERISA), the first major federal retirement plan legislation that recognized leveraged ESOPs, he continued to champion the ESOP cause. Before he retired in 1986, Congress passed 19 pieces of legislation promoting the ESOP cause.

HOW A LEVERAGED ESOP WORKS

The ESOP borrows money to buy either newly issued shares in the company or treasury shares to buy shares from existing owners. The company can then make tax deductible contributions to the ESOP to enable it to pay the loan off. As the loan is repaid, shares held by the ESOP are released and allocated to employee accounts.

TAX BENEFITS

There are several significant tax benefits available through an ESOP.

- Contributions to an ESOP are tax-deductible up to either 15 or 25 per cent of eligible pay. Eligible pay is defined under the IRS regulations to mean payment to employees as well as restrictions as to payment to senior executives. The higher limits apply to ESOPs combined with a money purchase pension plan, or ESOPs in closely held corporations (C corporations) that borrow money.

- Sellers to ESOPs in C corporations can defer any taxation they incur on the sale by reinvesting the proceeds in securities of domestic operating companies, provided they have held the stocks for at least three years. The ESOP must own 30 per cent or more of the company stock at or immediately following each transaction, and the ESOP ownership must not drop below 30 per cent within three years. Upon the death of a shareholder employee, the reinvested securities would receive a stepped-up basis of cost.

- Principal and interest on loans paid through an ESOP are tax-deductible.

- Dividends paid on ESOP shares and C corporations are tax-deductible when passed directly through to employees or used to repay any soft loan.

- In S corporations, the ESOP does not have to pay taxes on its pro rata profits. C corporations and S corporations are technical terms in the *Internal Revenue Services Act*.

HOW EMPLOYEES OWN STOCKS THROUGH ESOPs

Each employee meeting eligibility requirements (generally full-time employees with a year or more of service) participates in the plan and receives an allocation of stock each year. This is not compulsory, and employees may decline to join depending on their situation. Allocations of stock are subject to vesting, which means having the shares allocated by a transfer of legal title. The employee actually gets the shares after leaving the company. Closely held companies must repurchase the shares or have the ESOP do it.

HOW THE ESOP IS GOVERNED

The ESOP is governed by a trustee who must act for the exclusive benefit of participants. In closely held firms, employees are able to direct the trustee as to the voting and the shares, only on very limited issues; in publicly traded firms, votes pass through on all shareholder issues. The trustees can be any arm's-length party, either officers or directors of the company or third-party participants such as trust officers, bank officers, or lawyers. These issues are generally restricted to major changes in the nature or structure of the shareholdings of the company.

WHAT KIND OF EMPLOYER STOCK MUST THE ESOP HOLD

The ESOP must hold a publicly traded security in the company, or if there is no publicly traded security either the class of stock that has the highest combination of voting and dividend rights or preferred stock convertible into such stock. In other words, the employees must not be disadvantaged by being given a share of stock that has no economic value and is a sham.

EQUITY COMPENSATION PLANS

Many companies grant stock options to top management and key employees in order to link their interest with those of the shareholders. These are the golden handcuffs referred to previously in the book. In the past companies believed that these people make the greatest contribution to the company and, if they have a direct financial stake in how the company does, they will work to improve the company's performance.

Today, however, progressive companies understand that it takes a team effort to succeed. These companies consider all of their employees to be key and are looking for innovative ways to reward them for their service and contribution. In the last 10 years, there has been a dramatic increase in the number of companies granting stock options to a broad group of employees. Broad-based stock options are now the norm in high-technology companies and are becoming popular in many companies in other industries as part of an overall equity compensation strategy.

WHAT IS A STOCK OPTION?

A stock option is the right granted to an employee by a company to buy a given number of shares of company stock at stated price within a specified time period. It is not the same thing as a share of stock. A share represents an ownership interest in a company. Shareholders are entitled to vote on certain corporate matters, elect the firm's management, and receive any dividends declared by the board of directors. The grant of the stock option represents an opportunity for the employee to obtain shares of company stock when he or she exercises the option, and pays for the share of stock. Of course, there is no obligation to use the option, and the employee can simply allow it to lapse.

Why Stock Options are Valuable

The value of a stock option comes from its future appreciation. Individuals to whom options have been granted, called optionees, can lock in a set price for the shares, and then purchase these shares at a later date. With the stock option, employees have no financial obligation until they decide to buy company stock. If the stock price increases, the amount of gain (called the spread) between the current stock price and the original option price, will increase. Of course, the reverse is also possible.

How Employees Get Stock Options

The decision to grant options is made by the board of directors of a company. The grant can be based upon several criteria such as job category, years of continuous service with the company, merit, attainment of certain pre-targeted goals, and importance to the future direction of the company.

EXERCISE AND VESTING SCHEDULE

All options granted can be immediately exercisable or subject to a vesting schedule. Vesting, as previously stated, is the ability of the employee to be able to exercise the stock option and purchase shares. For example, a vesting schedule may stipulate the stock acquired upon exercise of options will vest at the rate of 20 per cent for each year of service so that all the shares will vest after five years. This means that certain restrictions on the stock will lapse at the rate of 20 per cent per year. So for example, after year one the employee will have 20 per cent of his or her stock vested. That 20 per cent then could be exercised by the employee and shares purchased. The other 80 per cent of the stock options would not yet be vested and could not be accessed until the schedule requirements are met.

HOW THE STOCK PRICE IS DETERMINED

The stock price of a company publicly traded is determined by what buyers will pay sellers for a stock on the public market, but a company that is non-publicly traded has to be valued in some other way. The terms of many plans require that the fair market value is determined by the board of directors based on independent valuations of the company. (Please see Chapter 5: Business Valuations.)

TYPE OF STOCK OPTIONS

There are two types of stock options: incentive stock options (ISOs) and non-qualified stock options (NSOs). An ISO allows an employee to not pay taxes at the time of the exercise and to pay only capital gains tax on the entirety. In order to qualify for this tax treatment certain conditions must be met. While ISOs are favorable to employees, companies cannot deduct the spread between the grant and the exercise price from their company's earnings. With NSOs, when an employee exercises the option, the spread between the grant and exercise price is taxable as ordinary income, regardless of whether the employee actually sells the shares. However, the company can deduct the spread from its earnings as a compensation expense. (Please see Chapter 6: Income Tax.)

EMPLOYEE STOCK PURCHASE PLANS

Some US employers believe that an ESOP is more meaningful to employees when they are required to purchase stock rather than having it given to them. This type of plan called the Section 423 Employee Stock Purchase Plan allows employees to receive certain tax benefits.

Statistical Profile of Employee Ownership

The National Centre for Employee Ownership (NCEO) in Oakland, California, collects statistical data on Employee Ownership Plans. It is a private, non-profit research organization that serves as the leading source of accurate, unbiased information on ESOPs, broadly granted employee stock options, and employee participation programs. The following statistical data is provided with the NCEO's permission. The table below shows the number of employee stock plans and the value of assets in these plans. It also shows the percentage of company stocks owned by different categories of employee ownership plans.

Percentage of Company Stock Owned by Employee Ownership Plans

Category	0–10%	11–30%	31–50%	50–100%
Private Company ESOPs	20%	35%	25%	20%
Public Company ESOPs	62%	34%	3%	1%
401K Plans	85%	10%	5%	0%
Stock Options	45%	53%	2%	0%

ESOPS' CORPORATE PERFORMANCE

The NCEO also conducts and compiles research on the relationship between employee ownership and corporate performance. Such studies are limited to ESOPs, both because data are easier to obtain on these companies and because they tend to be more committed to employee ownership than 401K plan sponsors, which tend to own relatively small amounts of the equity of individual companies.

The phenomenon of granting stock options to most or all employees is relatively recent and has not been reflected in studies of corporate performance. The principal findings on employee ownership and corporate performance is: *ESOPs and Corporate Growth: A 1987 NCEO Study of 45 ESOPs and 225 Non-ESOP Companies*, which found that companies that combine employee ownership with a participative management style grow 8 to 11 per cent per year faster than expected, based on past performance. Subsequent studies by the General Accounting Office and by academics in Washington State and New York found the same relationship. A 1999 study for Hewitt and Associates by Hammit Mehran of Northwestern University found that the return on assets for 382 publicly traded ESOP companies was 2.7 per cent per year greater than what a model of their predicted performance showed.

Studies on participative management alone find a small positive impact on performance. It is not nearly enough to explain the synergy between ownership and participation these other studies have found.

ESOPs and Stock Price Performance presents data compiled between 1992 and 1998 as part of an ongoing study by Joseph Blasi, Douglas Kruse, Michael Conte, and, after 1993, American Capital Strategies, which showed that an investment of equal amounts in a "shopping basket" of securities in public companies with more than 10 per cent broad employee ownership would see a return of 170 per cent compared to 143 per cent for the Dow Jones and 152 per cent for the S&P 500. The researchers point out that this does not establish causal linkage between employee ownership and stock performance because companies that set up these plans may also have certain other consistent features that make them perform better.

A 1995 study by Michael Conti at the University of Baltimore *ESOPs and Bankruptcy* found that during the 1980s fewer than one per cent of ESOPs were terminated because of the bankruptcy of the plan's sponsor.

Conclusion

The United States has over 25 years of ESOP experience and leads all other countries in terms of implementing and designing ESOPs. ESOP legislation has been consistently supported by both the Republican and the Democratic parties for over 25 years. In 1974 when the US was implementing its ESOP program, the Canadian and American rates of unemployment were roughly the same. Gradually, more employees in the United States became ESOP participants, the difference between the Canadian unemployment rate and the American unemployment rate grew substantially. Today the unemployment rate in Canada is between 6 and 8 per cent while in the United States its between 3 and 4 per cent.

EMPLOYEE SHARE OPTION PLANS IN THE UNITED KINGDOM

The United Kingdom has had a long and storied history in the growth of the rights of individuals. This respect for individual rights also created a desire to improve the economic rights of its citizens. ESOPs therefore have a long history in the United Kingdom with some experts identifying the start of employee share ownership as early as the nineteenth century.

Modern ESOPs arrived in the United Kingdom in 1989 under the tutelage of the Conservative Government of Margaret Thatcher. The privatization policies of the Thatcher government laid the political and social support needed to advance the ESOP through statutory authority. This was achieved with *The Finance Bill of 1989*, which allowed the tax deductibility of ESOP contributions. Additional amendments in April 1990 provided increased incentives for companies to implement ESOPs. These included allowing a company to guarantee to the bank the loans on behalf of the ESOP Trust. In March 1991, a beneficial rollover provision was added to the *Finance Act* allowing capital gains tax rollover relief for individuals selling stock to a statutory ESOP with at least 10 per cent employee ownership.

Even with these changes and amendments, ESOP implementation was slow to take hold under the legislation due to the strictness of the allocation and corporate governance rules.

Today the laws in the United Kingdom have been modified somewhat to allow the use of leveraged ESOPs similar to those in the United States. It is estimated by the ESOP Centre Limited that there are more than 2,000 companies operating ESOPs in the United Kingdom. This represents over three million employees, most of them employed in large public companies. In addition, the ESOP Centre Limited estimates that larger companies have ownership levels in the 4 to 5 per cent area, while smaller companies may have up to 20 per cent in employee ownership. A study done by the Centre in 1998 suggests that 75 per cent of the companies believe that ESOPs have had a positive impact in terms of both motivation and productivity.

The Employee Ownership Index ("EOI") as prepared by Capital Strategies, an independent corporate finance house based in the United Kingdom, has outperformed the FTSE All-Share Index (FTSE is a trademark of FTSE International) every year since 1992. In fact, an investment of £100 in the EOI in 1992 would be worth £800 in 2000, but only £251 in the FTSE All-Share Index. As the ESOP exists today in the United Kingdom, a company may choose to operate under a statutory authority or through an unapproved scheme. Due to the complexity of the laws it is important to obtain proper legal advice before implementing either a statutory or unapproved scheme.

RECENT DEVELOPMENTS

The New Labour Government of Tony Blair has committed itself to encouraging growth of ESOPs in the United Kingdom. In fact, Mr. Blair stated that his government wants to triple the number of ESOP Companies in the UK.

To achieve these goals, The Finance Act 2000 has created the following:

Company Share Option Plan

This scheme allows employees to be granted options by their companies with a value of up to a maximum of £30,000 on grant date per employee. These options must be granted at market value and there are strict rules governing the exercise of these options to avoid income taxes being paid immediately. The company has the right to choose which employees are granted options.

Approved Profit Sharing Scheme

This scheme allows a trust to buy shares in a company and to award them to employees at a later date. The trust obtains funds through a tax-deductible payment made by the company to the trust. Should the trust hold the shares for at least three years then the employee pays no income tax on the value of the free shares. Capital gains, however, are payable when the shares are sold.

Save As You Earn (SAYE) Sharesave

This scheme requires employees to save between £5 to £250 per month out of their post-tax pay. The employees are granted options to buy company shares at a discount of up to 20 per cent of the market value. The Employee Benefit Trust borrows money to buy the shares. Generally, employees are asked to sign saving contracts of three to seven years' duration. Employee gains upon exercise of the option are not subject to income tax provided the employee holds the shares until maturity of the contract. Problems can arise when companies are bought out as the employee must either exercise the option immediately and sell the shares or take back their savings plus interest.

Enterprise Management Incentive

This scheme involves new tax-shielded share options, which are granted with market value not to exceed £100,000. A company must have gross assets of less than £15 million and must be a private company. A maximum of £2.5 million may be allocated to key employees under such a scheme . This scheme was set up to address attraction and retention issues in high tech private companies. Should the key employees cash in after four years, the highest effective tax rate would be 10 per cent, and there are no income taxes charged on the exercise of the option.

All-Employee Ownership Plan

This scheme involves the introduction of three types of share plans:

- Partnership Shares: Employees can buy from pre-tax salary up to £1,500 of company stock or up to 10 per cent of salary, whichever is smaller at market value. These shares are free of tax at purchase.

- Matching Shares: Employees can be awarded by their company up to £3,000 worth of shares if they have bought Partnership Shares. Also free of tax.

- Free Shares: Employers may award up to £3,000 worth of free shares to employees per year free of tax. These shares may be subject to performance conditions.

As long as employees hold the above shares for at least five years, they are free of income tax. There is income tax payable at various rates if shares are cashed in before five years.

Conclusion

ESOPs are alive and well in the United Kingdom. Both government and corporations realize the huge impact ESOPs will have on the ability of the United Kingdom to compete in Europe and around the world. The recent *Finance Act 2000* will only accelerate the use and implementation of ESOPs in the United Kingdom.

APPENDIX I

Case Studies

T HIS SECTION INCLUDES publicly available information about employee share ownership plans and stock option plans in a number of Canadian and private companies. The examples are chosen to reflect the wide variety of firms—both in industry sector and size —that embrace the employee ownership concept.

The examples also reflect the status and development of employee share ownership in the two countries. The examples show a more evolved approach, as employee ownership is much more common in the United States.

The first nine case histories were compiled from information on the National Center for Employee Ownership (NCEO) web site www.nceo.org. They are used with permission.

A Business Software Company

(anonymous)

Ownership
Canadian-Controlled Private Corporation

Profile
The company is a Toronto-based information technology firm specializing in the design and delivery of strategic business software solutions, primarily for the financial services sector. Founded in 1990, the company has doubled in size every year.

Number of Employees
100+

Ownership Plan
An ESOP was introduced in 1995.

Employee Ownership/Participation
75 percent

Communications
The company instituted open-book management (OBM) under the fundamental premise that more knowledge means better performance. As part of the OBM strategy, the company presents monthly financial results and operating plans. There is also education regarding investment and the corporate financing and budgetary processes.

Plan Purpose
The goal of the ESOP was to attract and retain talented employees in a tight labour market. The company's voluntary attrition rate is under five percent in an industry where the norm is 20 to 25 percent.

An Electronic Component Sales and Distribution Company

(anonymous)

Ownership
Canadian-Controlled Private Corporation

Profile
The company is an award-winning high growth technology firm founded in 1988 by two principals. A parent company holds the original sales and distribution firm, a second company was acquired in 1995, and a new division was created in 1996.

Number of Employees
36

Ownership Plan
An ESOP was established in 1998. Participation is voluntary for employees who have been with the company for 12 consecutive months. The principals wanted to incorporate both stock purchase and gifting into the plan and so decided that for every two shares purchased, the employee would receive one stock option. The formula for allocation is tied to base salary as a percentage of total eligible-employee salary, times the total equity shares available.

Employee Ownership/Participation
Employees purchased 10 percent of company from treasury with a 98 percent participation rate. (The lone, eligible non-participant was leaving the company for personal reasons.)

Communications
Employees were made part of the process from the outset, with representation on the ESOP committee and through a questionnaire. An ongoing process of meetings and discussions created a constant feedback loop and information exchange between employer and employee. The process culminated with an information package for employees and a town hall meeting, an open Question and Answer forum for employees and their spouses.

Plan Purpose
The owners looked at an ESOP as a progressive way to share success with their employees and to solidify a commitment to growth. With plans for a public offering and global expansion, the company also looked to the ESOP as a means to attract and retain key people.

A Printing Company

(anonymous)

Ownership
Canadian-Controlled Private Corporation

Profile
The company was a union shop that had been owned by the same family for four decades. It was put up for sale in 1994.

Number of Employees
87

Ownership Plan
A management group proposed an ESOP and buyout in 1994, and profits have doubled every year since then. An open, consultative, and shared ownership culture encourages employee decision-making and accountability. Productivity has increased, and costs have been trimmed. Superior work has fostered customer loyalty.

Employee Ownership/Participation
95 percent participation

Communications
In preparation for the ESOP there was full disclosure to all employees. Employees had representation on the ESOP Committee, were polled by a questionnaire and participated in company-wide meetings and Question and Answer sessions. Communications are ongoing; the company president holds monthly information meetings for employees. When it is time to purchase shares, memos are circulated followed up with documents for those who request them.

Plan Purpose

For the employees, the ESOP provided a means to complete a leveraged buyout and pre-empt a possible sale and plant closure. For the owners it provided a succession plan.

A Communications and Entertainment Company

(anonymous)

Ownership

Canadian-Controlled Private Corporation

Profile

The company is a Toronto-based communications and entertainment firm providing creative business solutions that combine traditional and new media.

Number of Employees

200

Ownership Plan

The company has more than doubled since establishing an ESOP. The ESOP has been instrumental in helping grow the company into both a multi-national firm and one of the leaders in its field. The company has been able to maintain and cultivate an atmosphere of excitement, innovation, and community.

Employee Ownership/Participation

66 percent

Communications

The company has created an intranet site for employees with information on their plan. Employees can ask questions and receive specific answers. As a multi-national firm, the company has had to communicate the plans in different tax regimes.

Plan Purpose

With exploding growth, the owners needed to find innovative ways to manage success, to fuel growth and productivity.

Canadian Tire

Hard Goods Retailer

Ownership
Public

Profile
Canadian Tire is Canada's largest retailer of hard goods, with stores from coast to coast.

Number of Employees
38,000

Ownership Plan
Canadian Tire has four stock-based compensation plans. All full-time employees participate in profit-sharing and a stock purchase/matching program. Certain employees are granted options, and there is a Deferred Share Unit Plan (DSUP) provision for members of the board of directors, which allows them to elect to take all or part of their annual compensation in the form of notional Class A non-voting shares.

Employee Ownership/Participation
80 percent of eligible employees (3,200 participating)

Communications
The stock purchase plan is part of the new employee orientation. Ongoing communications include a quarterly statement to participating employees outlining what has been paid, and disposed as well as current market value, with information provided by their independent record-keeper. Also, the employees' bi-weekly pay stub shows the withholding amount for the pay period and the year to date.

Plan Purpose
The plans are incentives for performance and profitability through employee ownership. The plan supplements other in-company capital plans and contributes towards employees' long term retirement security. Employees receive bonuses at the end of year based on how much they contribute. For example, if the employee contributes $3,000 over the year, the company will match 50 percent, or $1,500 in this example,

to buy additional shares. The bonus shares cannot be sold or withdrawn immediately—they must be held on a sliding scale over 10 years. Also, the company pays the tax on the 50 percent bonus shares. Dividends are also used to purchase additional shares.

SNC-Lavalin Group
Engineering and Construction

Ownership
Public

Profile
SNC-Lavalin is one of the world's leading engineering and construction companies with offices throughout Canada and in 30 other Countries. In the 1950s SNC was a partnership of 130 people. It became a limited company in 1966, which opened up more growth capital.

Number of Employees
10,000

Ownership Plan
In addition to employee ownership provisions, in 1995, the company adopted a stock option plan under which it may grant options to non-employee directors and certain key employees up to the limit permitted by law. Options be exercised only two years after the date of grant, at the market value of the shares on the date of grant for a period not exceeding five years. Except in the cases of death or company-approved retirement, options terminate upon cessation of employment or resignation.

Employee Ownership/Participation
20 percent

Communications
When the ESOP was implemented in 1996 communications were sent out to all employees describing the provisions of the plan. The ESOP is part of the compensation plan described in the employee handbook. Ongoing communications include a quarterly statement issued by the

fiduciary to participating employees of the plan. Also, the employees' bi-weekly pay stub shows the withholding amount for the pay period and the year-to-date withholding amount.

Plan Purpose
The idea behind employee-ownership was to motivate people to initiate ideas and actions, to be business leaders, and to go out and get contracts for the company. A former CEO says employee ownership created a team spirit and made employees proud of what they were doing.

Algoma Steel
Steel Manufacturer

Ownership
Public

Profile
Algoma is a 90-year-old steel manufacturer, Canada's third-largest producer, located in Sault Ste.Marie, Ontario.

Number of Employees
4100

Ownership Plan
In 1992, the United Steel Workers of America (USWA) spearheaded a buy-out of the company which was then in financial difficulty. It took a year to settle all the details, but ultimately the workers ended up with 60 percent ownership. Today employees own or exercise control over roughly 24 percent of the outstanding shares. When the buyout plan was set up in 1992, there were two trusts, one for unionized employees and one for salaried employees. Montreal Trust is the registered holder of the shares.

Employee Ownership/Participation
24 percent ownership

Communications
Communications continue to be a top priority at Algoma. Unionized

employees are full partners in the company's management and decision-making process. As members on a joint strategic planning committee, they are responsible for jointly managing business processes and objectives, business plans, and goals. Estimates are that between 1993 and 1995 alone, employee suggestions accounted for $7 million in immediate savings, with longer-term implications.

Plan Purpose
The plan was initiated to keep the company in business and prevent loss of jobs.

APPENDIX II

Sample ESOP Engagement Letter

Re: ESOP Implementation At X-Tech Inc.

Dear Ms N...:

We are pleased to present our proposal regarding the design, installation, and communication of an Employee Share Ownership Plan (ESOP) at X-Tech Inc. in a manner that meets your corporate vision and ensures that the ESOP is aligned successfully into your existing corporate culture and structure over the long term.

The main purpose of the ESOP is to attract and retain star performers, which will allow the company to expand and capture a larger percentage of the market share quickly and efficiently.

Background

You requested that we quote on a timely delivery and management of the ESOP transaction. The approach we will use will transition your existing organization to one with an ESOP as its base, where everyone not only acts like an owner but also could in fact be an owner.

Our mission statement is to make shared ownership a profitable reality. We are uniquely suited to accomplish this task for the following reasons:

- ESOPs are our specialty, and our company was established to deliver the design, implementation, and communication of ESOPs;

- Seven years experience in Canadian ESOP design, implementation, and communication;

- Clients are knowledge-based companies with a highly skilled and mobile work force;

- Specialize in small and medium-sized private corporations with high sales growth;

- Flexible in that we can provide the components for the ESOP in-house, including ESOP design, business valuation, and tax planning or work with professional advisors of your choice;

- Our model we for implementing ESOPs includes strategies outlined in a Blueprint and communication documents (such as question-naires and summaries);

- Value-added services including ESOP financing, personal financial planning, ESOP administration, communications, and open-book management.

Objectives of a Successful ESOP

- Attract and retain the people who drive the success of the company with a view to enhancing the proposed high-performance company direction;

- Integrate the ESOP into the corporate culture;

- Create increased value for current owners through increased intel-lectual asset value as well as higher employee productivity and morale with lower turnover;

- Achieve a high employee participation rate in the ESOP;

- Reward employees for current, past, and future contributions.

The ESOP Transformation Model©

The ESOP Transformation Model©, which we have developed and used for the benefit of our clients, is transaction-oriented. Our goal is to pro-duce the best available plan, which meets owner, corporate, and employee objectives under budget and in reasonable time frame.

A typical assignment involves three phases, including ESOP Diagnos-tics and Design, ESOP Communications, and ESOP Implementation. Within these three Phases, major components such as ESOP structur-ing, business valuation, tax, and other issues are reviewed and imple-mented. See page 187 for an outline of the steps in each of these components.

Deliverables

The deliverables involved in the ESOP process include:

- ESOP plan design and strategy

- Confirming ESOP participants and ESOP team

- Critical path

- Employee questionnaire and feedback

- Blueprint document (detailed analysis of ESOP design)

- Communication program

- Tax-minimization plan

- Valuation

- ESOP summary document

- Attendance at Town Hall meeting

Staffing

The ESOP diagnostic, design, and tax components are provided by ESOP Builders Inc. The business valuation is provided by firm ABC. The project will be managed by Mr. J. Abe, president, and Mr. D. Dow, director of client services.

Fees and Timing

The professional fees for the core components can be broken down into three Phases as follows:

	Phase I $	Phase II $	Phase III $	Total $
ESOP Diagnostics & Design				
Business valuation				
Tax structure				

Total

Generally Phase I involves:

- points 1 to 6 listed in the Diagnostics and Design (D&D) section on page 187 (e.g., meetings, draft Blueprint, questionnaire);

Generally Phase II involves:

- points 7 to 9 in the D&D section (final Blueprint, ESOP Summary); points 1 to 4 in the Valuation section (draft valuation report); and points 6 to 9 in the Tax section (review and summary of tax structure);

Generally Phase III involves:

- points 9 and 10 in the D&D section (Town Hall, employee feedback, and post-ESOP options); and point 5 in the Valuation section (final valuation report).

Please note that the above fixed fee breakdown is for only the portions of the project outlined in this proposal (ESOP Diagnostics and Design, Valuation, and Tax structure). You may also choose to obtain fee quotes from your professional advisors for the valuation and tax components.

The ESOP transaction will likely require the preparation of legal documents (i.e., shareholders' agreement and forms). We can recommend a law firm with which we have worked with on other ESOPs, or you may prefer to use your own legal advisors.

Please also note that should we be required to raise capital for your employees to purchase shares, we will charge a separate fee for the amount raised. Should you require other capital funding, we will also quote on a separate basis.

We would bill all reasonable disbursements incurred on this assignment separately at cost. These would be approximately 3 percent of the project cost.

It is our policy to request at signing, a retainer of approximately 50 percent of the estimated fee for Phase I of the work, plus GST. We would render interim billings over the period of the project with the final account at the time of completion of the final report. All billings are payable upon receipt. Should circumstances arise that might materially affect our time and cost, we would discuss the matter with you first and take direction accordingly.

We confirm that all materials provided by you and your company are confidential and will be used solely in relation to the ESOP assignment. We will sign any confidentiality agreement pursuant to this representation.

If you wish to proceed with this ESOP project, please sign this letter where indicated below and attach a retainer cheque in the amount of $X,XXX. Upon receipt, we will proceed with the assignment.

Thank you for the opportunity to work with you on this most important assignment.

Yours truly,

Consultant Firm

President

You are hereby authorized to proceed in accordance with the above terms of reference for the ESOP activities:

_____   _____
Name   Title

_____   _____
Company   Date

Components of the ESOP Process

The Overall ESOP Diagnostics and Design Component

1. The consultant will identify key drivers, goals, and issues for the ESOP from management's perspective. We review current incentive and communication structures to ensure they will mesh with a new ESOP. Further issues to consider:

   a. Financing the ESOP transaction fees through the employee purchase;

   b. Financing for the ESOP share purchase by the employees;

2. The consultant will develop a critical path essential to meeting ESOP deadlines.

3. The consultant will work with management to design, refine, and strengthen the ESOP. Also included would be the establishment of an ESOP team including management, external advisors, and employee representatives. The team would then be involved with planning sessions as required.

4. In tandem, we solicit feedback on the concept of ESOPs by initiating employee communications through customized questionnaires, contact groups, and internal media;

5. This feedback is used to address employee concerns while maintaining a focus on achieving management's goals. This part of the process is critical to achieving a high participation rate and must be well planned and executed to achieve desirable results.

6. The ESOP is documented in a Blueprint, outlining the design of the ESOP including technical and financial considerations. This Blueprint is used as the template for creation of the legal agreements and deals with specific ESOP parameters as they apply to the company such as:

   a. *ESOP objectives and strategy;*

   b. *share percentage, distribution, allocation and attributes, eligibility, stock options versus stock equity, key versus non-key persons, vesting period, forfeiture, purchase formula, purchase methods, investment methods (RRSPs), pricing, buyout conditions, exit strategies, information disclosure policies.*

7. The ESOP is outlined in layman's terms to the employees in an ESOP Summary based upon the Blueprint and legal documents.

8. An Employee Information Package is assembled and distributed to all eligible employees explaining the ESOP in detail.

9. A company Town Hall Meeting is held to introduce and discuss the ESOP with the employees.

10. Assess employee feedback and post-ESOP options and strategy. Further issues for management to consider at this point include:

   a. Post-ESOP communications program;

   b. Internal ESOP administration and documentation;

   c. Realignment of existing and future incentive/benefit plans;

   d. Personal financial and tax planning;

   e. Business literacy and open-book management;

   f. ESOP management style;

   g. Developing a corporate ESOP culture.

The Valuation and Tax Components

In order to operate an ESOP company, a business valuation is required on an annual basis to determine the fair market value of the employee shares. ESOP Builders Inc. can provide the annual valuation, which would include the following:

1. A review of the past and current financial position as well as financial projections for subsequent years;

2. A review of corporate operations including interviews and correspondence with management and other professional advisers in order to augment our knowledge of the operations of the company;

3. A review of published market data and research related to your industry as well as relevant trends in the industry and economy;

4. A draft valuation report outlining the valuation approach, assumptions, and support for the conclusion;

5. A final report, with an abbreviated summary available for employees if required.

In order for the ESOP to be structured in a tax-effective manner both from a corporate and personal perspective, a review of the current tax situation and corporate structure is recommended. This would entail the following:

6. A review of the corporate structure with a view to maximizing tax efficiency of the plan;

7. A review of the share structure with a view to the future requirements of the ESOP and the current status of the company owners;

8. A review of the existing tax regime to assure compliance of the ESOP with the current legislation and ensure maximum use of benefits available for the company and employees;

9. A final narration outlining the tax structure of the ESOP.

Initial Information and Documents Required

1. Number of employees, broken down into departments and pay scales;

2. Details on profit-sharing plans, incentive plans, benefit plans etc.;

3. Company procedures and policies;

4. Outline of corporate decision-making process;

5. Any studies or reports on the company done within the last three years and details of any ongoing or planned management consultant studies and related activities;

6. Key-person insurance and other relevant policies;

7. Copy of employment contracts with key individuals;

8. Contact names, including key individuals, external advisors etc.;

9. Corporate and share structure;

10. History of share transactions including amount, price, and names of parties involved in the transactions;

11. Banking agreements;

12. Previous valuations of the company (verbal or written);

13. Federal and provincial tax returns for the last two years;

14. Last five years of financial statements and the latest interim statements;

15. Forecasts or budget financial statements;

16. Client contracts or agreements;

17. Industry background (names of associations, periodicals).

Sample Critical Path Milestones

Week 1   Receive documents; initial meeting; all project team members to be confirmed; scope ESOP design; communication strategy.

Week 2   Establish transition team; first team meeting; develop critical path; allocate responsibilities.

Weeks 3–4   Valuation; tax strategy; agreements in draft; draft Blueprint of ESOP; stock plan.

Week 5   ESOP questionnaire.

Weeks 6–7	Transition team meeting; feedback from ESOP questionnaire; ESOP presentation.
Weeks 8–9	Preliminary Information Package.
Weeks 10–11	Finalize all documents.
Weeks 12–13	Town Hall meeting; subscription meeting.
Week 14	Closing of ESOP transaction.

APPENDIX III

Sample ESOP Questionnaire

Your employer would like to implement an Employee Share Ownership Plan (ESOP) for employees within the company.

An ESOP is a plan that may include ownership of stock equity (shares) of a company. An ESOP allows employees to participate and benefit financially in the future growth of the company through ownership.

In preparation for this ESOP, we are asking the employees to please answer the following questions as completely as possible and return this form by June 30 to___. Your input is valuable to us and will help in designing the plan and addressing your questions and concerns. We understand that you do not yet have enough information about the ESOP for a personal evaluation, but the responses will provide us with a sense as to general employee interest and understanding. The ESOP will be formally introduced at a company meeting in August and you will also be provided with documentation outlining the plan.

This questionnaire is confidential so you do not have to provide your name. Your individual responses will remain confidential, and only consolidated information will be provided to management for their consideration in the design of the company ESOP.

ESOP Builders Inc. is assisting in the design of the plan and we ask that you please send your responses directly to Ian McDowell by fax to 905 625-8431.

SAMPLE

CONFIDENTIAL – ESOP QUESTIONNAIRE

Please mark the appropriate answer:

1. Do you understand what is meant by the following terms:

ESOP	**Yes**	**No**
Stock equity (shares)	**Yes**	**No**
Stock options	**Yes**	**No**
Self-directed RRSP	**Yes**	**No**
Profit sharing	**Yes**	**No**

	Strongly Agree	Somewhat Agree	Strongly Disagree	Do not know
2. An ESOP is a valuable employee benefit.	1 2	3	4 5	0
3. An ESOP will be a competitive advantage for our company.	1 2	3	4 5	0
4. I would rather be employed at a privately owned company that has an ESOP.	1 2	3	4 5	0
5. I understand how companies like ours may increase in value over the next few years.	1 2	3	4 5	0
6. If I had a choice, I would rather receive stock options over a cash bonus.	1 2	3	4 5	0
7. If I had a choice, I would rather receive stock equity (shares) over a cash bonus.	1 2	3	4 5	0

8. If I had a choice, I would:

   a. purchase stock equity   1   2   3   4   5   0

   b. receive stock options   1   2   3   4   5   0

   c. purchase shares and
      receive stock options   1   2   3   4   5   0

9. Which of the following benefits would be of most interest to you. Rank in order from 1 to 10:

   __ Bonus

   __ Education subsidies

   __ Flexible hours

   __ Group RRSP

   __ Personal financial planning

   __ Personal fitness programs

   __ Profit sharing

   __ Stock equity (shares)

   __ Stock options

   __ Other (please comment) _____

10.a. If offered shares in this company, would you purchase them (assuming all your questions and concerns have been addressed)?

        Yes   **No**   **Do not know**

   b. If yes, how much would you likely invest annually?

      Less than $1,000   **$1,000–$2,000**

      $2,001 – $5,000   **Greater than $5,000**

11. How would you likely fund the purchase?

Company bonus	Yes	No	**Do not know**
RRSP contribution	Yes	No	**Do not know**
Existing RRSP holdings	Yes	No	**Do not know**
Payroll deduction	Yes	No	**Do not know**
Bank loan	Yes	No	**Do not know**
Cash	Yes	No	**Do not know**
Other (specify)	Yes	No	**Do not know**

12. a. Do you own Registered Retirement Savings Plans (RRSPs)?

    Yes   **No**   **Do not know**

 b. If yes to 12a, is your RRSP a self-directed Plan?

    Yes   **No**   **Do not know**

 c. Would you consider using a self-directed RRSP in order to hold shares in the company?

    Yes   **No**   **Do not know**

13. Do you believe *all current* employees should be eligible to receive shares and/or stock options?

    Yes   **No**   **Do not know**

14. Do you believe *all future* employees should be eligible to receive shares and/or stock options?

    Yes   **No**   **Do not know**

15. If you would NOT consider joining the ESOP, please indicate your reasons:

_____

_____

16. Think forward four years and imagine what could have taken place that made you glad you still worked at this company (Briefly describe).

_____

_____

17. Based upon your personal knowledge, do you have any questions, concerns, or comments specific to a share purchase or stock option plan at the company:

_____

_____

18. How long do you think you will stay with the company?

      __ Less than 1 year

      __ 1 – 3 years

      __ 3 – 5 years

      __ 5 – 10 years

      __ longer than 10 years

19. What would likely extend your career within the company?

_____

_____

Thank you for your input.
Consultant Firm
Name of individual

APPENDIX IV

Frequently Asked Questions

(Some specific values and percentages have been used for example purposes.) Outlined below is a list of the most common questions asked about ESOPs.

1) Is participation mandatory?

    a) No. Your position with the company does not depend upon your participation in the program.

2) Who are eligible for the shares?

    a) Generally, all full-time regular employees who were employed with [the company] up to [specify date] are eligible for the ESOP. Generally all full-time employees hired after that date would have a six-month waiting period before becoming eligible. The Board will determine whether employees who have satisfied these employment criteria are to be classified as a Designated Person, an Eligible Person or a New Eligible Person. The Board of Directors will also have the ultimate discretion as to whether anyone can be excluded from participation. Contract personnel are not eligible.

3) Who decides how many shares an employee can buy?

    a) The Board of Directors allocates shares for each employee and manages the program.

4) Is seniority a factor in the allocation of shares?

    a) Employees who have been employed prior to [specify date] get a one-time bonus allocation.

5) How do we know that the method of allocation is fair?

    a) The Board of Directors has used a salary formula for uniformity. The management also has to ensure that individuals who are key to the future success and value of the company are rewarded adequately. This has been done by developing different classifications with different share allocations.

6) **Are we eligible to transfer shares or options into a RRSP or 401(k)?**

   a) The shareholders' Agreement does permit the transfer of shares to an RRSP, and you cannot hold options within an RRSP. For US employees, the company shares can be transferred into your 401(k) but options cannot.

7) **Can we use money other than our bonus if we choose to acquire shares under the Share Acquisition Plan?**

   a) No. The Board wants to ensure that the employees earn the shares through the bonus program at this time.

8) **Can we buy more shares than our bonus will pay for?**

   a) No. You can acquire only up to the number of shares that have been allocated for you. This could be below or above your bonus amount. The company has allowed participants up to[   ]to use their bonus to acquire shares.

9) **When will the company go public and on what exchange?**

   a) Our current objective is to go public within the foreseeable future. However there are no guarantees. The exchange will probably be the TSE but it could also be NASDAQ. You will be kept informed of our progress towards this goal.

10) **How much of the share offering would be made available to the public?**

   a) This ESOP offering is for employees only and, no shares will be made available to the public.

11) **Do our shares have any value before we go public?**

   a) Yes, but there are limited ways to realize the value, as detailed in the shareholders' agreement. For example, upon death, your estate would receive fair market value, and upon termination you would receive 75 percent of fair market value.

12) **How do I liquidate the shares if the company does not go public?**

   a) If the company does not go public or sell to a third party, you can sell shares only according to the special circumstances described in the shareholder agreement.

13) **How long do we have to hold the shares after we go public?**

   a) That depends upon which exchange and their restrictions. Generally, you may have to hold them for a period of 0 to 365 days, or more in special circumstances.

14) **How is the share price/option price determined?**

   a) The Board of Directors determines the fair market value of the shares and options through consultation with its accountants, [name of firm]. The value will be generally determined annually by the Board of Directors.

15) **What is the initial value of the shares and the terms to acquire them?**

   a) Each common share will initially be $100.00. Your bonus will be used to acquire common shares, which also entitles you to receive stock options. However, you do not have to pay anything for the stock options.

16) **When are the shares/options offered and exercised?**

   a) This offer will be made on [date]. However, you can acquire your shares up to [date]. The options are immediately vested, and you have up to five years to exercise them. For new employees, shares with matching options will also be provided under this program.

17) **Are the shares/options better than the cash equivalent? How do you compare them?**

   a) We are not qualified to give investment advice, and you must do your own analysis of the offer.

   However, Canadian employees acquiring shares do not pay tax on that amount until the shares are sold. You also receive a stock option. If you were to take a cash bonus instead of shares, you would have income tax withheld. However, as with any investment, there is a risk of losing your investment.

US employees receiving a cash bonus pay tax when receiving the cash benefit. When you receive shares or options the receipt of shares/options will be subject to tax before you receive the cash benefit from the proceeds of selling the shares.

18) **What happens if a third party buys the company?**

a) You would receive your pro rata portion of the proceeds of the sale.

19) **How much financial information will be available before I decide to buy?**

a) The company will provide a summary of historical and current results.

20) **Will we see financial statements every year?**

a) Yes, a summary financial report will be presented annually.

21) **Can we cash out our shares at any time?**

a) No. Your shares can be sold to the company only in certain circumstances, such as death or termination, based upon the shareholders' agreement.

22) **Can we change the percentage of our bonus used to acquire shares?**

a) No. The percentage of your bonus to be received in shares cannot be changed. Once you have acquired your elected amount of shares, the remainder of your bonus (if any) will be paid in cash.

23) **What happens to our shares if we leave the company?**

a) If you leave the company, it may purchase your shares at the company's option. If you leave as a result of death, disability, or retirement, you will receive fair market value (FMV). As a result of bankruptcy or termination, you receive 75 percent of FMV. All stock options that are vested at the time of death, disability, or retirement must be exercised within 180 days of leaving the company, and the company has the right to buy back the shares. All stock options that are vested at time of termination must be exercised within 30 days of leaving the company, and the company has the right to buy back the shares.

24) Do the shares have voting rights?

a) All the shares are common shares with full voting rights.

25) Will we get dividends?

a) If dividends are declared on common shares, you will receive your allocation. However, since we are a growing company that needs to reinvest its capital in technology and staff, we will not likely pay dividends.

26) Is there a limit on the percentage of shares held by individuals?

a) There is a 5 percent limit on individual ownership of shares.

27) What are the risks of investing in the company?

a) As with any investment, there is the risk of loss. The company could potentially go bankrupt, in which case your investment would be lost. The company is not public; therefore there is no liquidity to your shares. The company is relatively small and must compete against larger and better-capitalized competitors.

28) What proportion of my bonus can I use to acquire shares?

a) You may elect 0, 25, 50, 75, or 100 percent of your bonus as cash with the dollar value of the balance used to acquire shares.

29) What if we go public before I acquire all my shares?

a) It is the company's intention to make all reasonable efforts to create the opportunity for all employees to have acquired all of their shares under the Share Acquisition Plan prior to going public subject to regulatory requirements.

APPENDIX V
EMPLOYEE BLUEPRINT
EMPLOYEE SHARE OWNERSHIP PLAN (ESOP)

CONFIDENTIAL DRAFT

FOR DISCUSSION ONLY

This is a summary of what is anticipated to be in the Employee Information Package. A review of this material should not be a substitute for the examination of the final Employee Information Package.

DRAFT
EMPLOYEE BLUEPRINT SUMMARY
TABLE OF CONTENTS

INTRODUCTION

DEFINITIONS

ESOP PURPOSE AND GOALS

ESOP PARAMETERS

CRITICAL PATH

EMPLOYEE BLUEPRINT

INTRODUCTION

An Employee Share Ownership Plan (ESOP) is a method by which a portion of the company ownership is transferred from the existing shareholders to the employees.

This document outlines the ESOPs' major features and will provide an introduction to the ESOP. It is not the final detailed legal document.

The company will be introducing an ESOP for employees of these companies, to enable them to acquire common shares of the company.

An Employee Information Package describing the ESOP in detail will be provided to you as soon as possible prior to a town hall meeting. You should read the Package carefully before making your decision whether to purchase shares. You should not rely solely upon this document.

This is a one-time share offer to the employees. All eligible company employees (described below) will be able to purchase common shares from the ESOP.

DEFINITIONS

i.   Eligible Employees—all full-time regular employees of the company (excluding company founders) who have been employed for six months as of the end of the past year;

ii. Pool A—the shares in Pool A (also referred to as the stock or equity pool) are common voting shares and will be sold to eligible employees;

iii. Pool B—the shares in Pool B (also referred to as the option pool) are to be used as stock options. One stock option will be automatically granted for every two Pool A shares purchased. The compensation committee can also allocate additional stock options to employees;

iv. Stock (or Share) Purchase—A stock (or share) purchase is an actual sale of stock (or shares) to the employee with the transfer of title upon payment. Shares are an accepted industry standard of compensation for employees because they reflect the ability of the employee to influence future growth and value of the company;

v. Stock Option—A stock option is a right conferred by the company upon an employee to purchase shares of the company at some future date, at a fixed price, at the discretion of the employee. Stock options are an accepted industry standard of compensation for employees because they reflect the ability of the employee to influence future growth and value of the company;

vi. Compensation Committee— Initially to be made up of founding owners. This committee will be responsible for allocating stock purchases (via formula) and stock options;

vii. Fair Market Value (FMV)—For purposes herein, we have taken the term "fair market value" to mean the highest price, expressed in terms of money or money's worth, obtainable in an open and unrestricted market between informed and prudent parties, acting at arm's length, neither party being under any compulsion to transact.

viii. Vesting Period—The amount of time that has to pass before the stock option can be exercised (and shares subsequently purchased).

ESOP PURPOSE AND GOALS

The ESOP is being formed for the financial and organizational benefit of the company's employees first, the company, its customers, and suppliers second, and the current ownership third.

For the employees, the ESOP will provide:

a. The opportunity to participate in the long-term growth and increased value of the company;

b. Ownership of the underlying assets and future potential of the company; and

c. Potential for individual tax planning.

For the company, the ESOP will:

a. Help to keep and attract key personnel, which will encourage innovation and company growth;

b. Facilitate widespread ownership, decreasing risk to potential investors and increasing the value of the company; and

c. Encourage employees to participate and work towards creating a high-performance company capable of superior productivity, profits, and value and increase commitment of all employees to the common goals of the company.

For the customers and suppliers, the ESOP will:

a. Improve supplier relationships as suppliers will be dealing with employee owners; and

b. Increase customer and supplier satisfaction and retention through improved communication with employee owners.

For the current owners, the ESOP will:

a. Allow for an expansion of the company; and

b. Help the employees to understand the business and how to increase value for all shareholders.

ESOP PARAMETERS

1. Starting Date

The start date, for purposes of share allocation, will be [date], and all employees who have been employed by the company for at least six months as of this date will be eligible for the share purchase through the ESOP. The ESOP transaction will close [date] and all share purchases must be completed by this date.

All shares sold to the employees will be issued from the company treasury stock. As a result, all funds raised from the sale of shares to the employees will go back into the company for corporate expansion.

2. Initial Public Offering (IPO)

The longer-term strategy for the company, as for many private companies, may be to eventually become a publicly traded corporation. If this occurs, the company would sell shares to the public on a public stock exchange. The advantages of becoming a publicly traded corporation are access to financing for more rapid company growth, increased exposure to the public market place for product sales, and potential increases in share value for the current shareholders (the ESOP and original owners). There is currently no intention for the company to go public in the near future.

When a private company decides to sell shares to the public for the first time, it does so by an Initial Public Offering (IPO) through a recognized stock exchange (e.g., Toronto Stock Exchange, Alberta Stock Exchange, etc.). A company going public needs to offer enough shares to float or issue to the public to make it an attractive investment to investors. This amount will be determined at the time of the IPO, but usually between 30 percent and 40 percent of the shares will be sold to the public. Since the public issue will dilute existing shareholdings, the current and future employee shareholders will want to maintain control of a large portion of the shares after the IPO so that the company can continue to follow its business and marketing plans in order to reach its goals.

Generally, public investors will also want to see the original owners and employees with a significant stake in the company because this shows their commitment to the success of the company.

3.   ESOP Share Issue

To account for growth of the company, and to attract quality employees and maintain a motivated work force, we have developed the following parameters in deciding the amount of shares which can be issued to the employees. These are as follows:

• The number of employees could double or triple over the next several years;

• Some type of bonus must be created through share purchase and share options for motivating employees;

- A share purchase formula must recognize contributions of existing and future employees; and

- There must be a pool of shares available that is big enough to attract key personnel.

Based upon the above parameters, an ESOP allocation pool will be created for the following reasons:

- To allow enough room to accommodate future employees; and

- Flexibility to change strategy if future financing needs change.

- The advantages of this allocation are:

- Sufficient wealth-creation opportunity to be attractive and motivational;

- Flexible, so that if circumstances change, allocation can be revised to meet the change; and

- Allows for exceptional growth in the number of employees over next three years.

4.   Assumptions for the ESOP

The following assumptions have been made in order to set up the initial Plan:

- ESOP close date [   ] ;

- Shares allocated for purchase by all eligible employees are based upon a pre-determined formula; and

- Stock option shares granted to all eligible employees.

5.   Basis of Allocation

- Stock allocation:

ESOP shares are to be allocated to employees based upon a salary formula (see Formula for Purchase of Shares);

- Stock options:

One stock option will be automatically granted for every two shares purchased by an employee. The compensation committee can also allocate additional stock options to employees.

6. Share Structure

A share in a company is like a share in anything else: it is a piece of the pie. Since shares have a fairly small unit value, they are rather small pieces, but if the pie grows big enough, then even a relatively small percentage of shares can have a meaningful increase in value.

The ESOP will be issued common shares. Common shares are "growth" shares—they grow in value as the value of the company grows (or decrease in value as the value of the company decreases).

Common shares carry certain attributes such as voting rights and rights to receive dividend distributions (which may be paid at the discretion of the Board of Directors). There is however, no intention to pay dividends at this time.

7. Eligibility

The overall ESOP goal is to reward long-term commitment to the company and superior performance.

The ESOP will be a combination of stock purchase and stock options. This allows maximum flexibility to meet changing circumstances in the market place.

Full-time regular employment for a period of six months, as of [date], will be required before being eligible to purchase ESOP shares. This period was chosen due to the nature of the training cycle within the company and the length of time it takes to judge the success of an individual within the corporate culture of the company.

As an eligible employee, you will have the right to purchase shares (and receive the automatically granted stock options) subject to the above and based upon a formula (outlined in the section below).

The compensation committee may also allocate additional stock options based upon merit (some criteria are outlined in the section below). Participation in ESOP is not a right of the employee but rather must be earned. Stock options can be offered at any time and are not limited to the six-month employment minimum. It is the compensation committees' intention to identify these employees on an annual basis.

8. Formula for Purchase of Shares (Pool A) and Granting of Stock Options (Pool B)

The overall goal is to create a fair allocation while at the same time recognizing superior performance and contribution.

The compensation committee is responsible for:
a. Calculating the formula for the stock purchase by all employees; and

b. Granting of stock options to employees.

Employee Stock Purchase Formula (Pool A) (*excludes founding shareholders*):

The formula for stock purchase distribution will be based upon employee salary:

(Employee's annual salary/ Total payroll of all eligible participants*) X # of shares in pool A = A

*(excluding original owner salaries)
A = Employee Share Allocation
Example: (figures are used for example only)
Employee's salary = $50,000
Total payroll = $1,000,000
# of shares in Pool A = 60,000
Calculation of number of shares eligible for purchase:
(50,000/1,000,000) X 60,000 = 3,000 shares

Stock Options (Pool B)

There will be one stock option automatically granted for every two shares purchased. The compensation committee can also allocate additional stock options based upon factors such as:

a. Job responsibility;

b. Potential for growth;

c. Value to company;

d. Contribution to company growth;

e. Future impact on value growth of company;

f. New business development;

g. New product development;

h. Strategic input; and

i. Importance to a potential IPO.

9. Vesting Period for Stock Options

Stock options are vested equally over a three-year period, subject to exercising a maximum of 33.33 percent of the option per year. If an employee leaves the company, the stock option lapses (unless there are extenuating circumstances as directed by the Board of Directors; see Buyout Conditions).

10. Purchase Methods

The employee will be entitled to purchase shares using his/her own personal funds. However, the company recognizes that employees may not have the resources for such an investment. As such, the company will allow the employee to use his/her bonus and/or commission towards the purchase. Purchasing shares gives the employee a real stake in the risks and rewards in the future of the company.

11. Tax Structure

This structure will be outlined in the separate Information Package and will be prepared by [name of firm], who will outline the technical details and show the pros and cons of various tax scenarios.

12. How to Shelter Your Investment

In Canada, the federal government has set up a plan designed to allow individuals to save money and defer paying any taxes until after they retire. This plan is called a RRSP. It allows an individual to invest up to 18 percent of eligible income in a RRSP and not pay any tax until the money is withdrawn by the plan holder.

You may be able to put your ESOP share purchase into this type of plan and receive a tax deduction against your income.

In order to be eligible to put the shares into a RRSP, it must be registered as a self-directed RRSP.

A deferral of tax is available with respect to a gain on a sale of the shares or dividends received if the shares are held in a RRSP. The shares have to meet certain qualifications to be eligible as a RRSP investment. The company shares may currently qualify for RRSP purposes but circumstances could change this status in the future.

There is a $500,000 lifetime capital gains exemption that may be available on a future sale of the shares. However, in order to qualify for this exemption, you have to retain shares personally for at least two years and not shelter them in your RRSP. There are several other qualifications that have to be met in order to claim the exemption.

The future exercise of the stock options to acquire shares results in a taxable benefit. However, this benefit can be delayed for tax purposes until the shares are sold. Although employees may not want to exercise their stock options until the shares will be sold, there are circumstances where it may be beneficial to exercise the options prior to the sale of the shares.

The ESOP provides for the employees to sell the shares back to the company in certain circumstances. In most cases this sale to the company will result in a deemed taxable dividend and a capital loss. The sale of the shares to anyone other than the company will result in a capital gain or loss. Capital gains are included in income at a 50 percent rate. Capital losses, at the 50 percent rate, can be deducted against other capital gains.

13. Valuation

A valuation of the company is necessary in order to determine the price at which the employees can buy or sell shares. Unlike a public company where the shares are traded every day on a stock exchange at whatever the value the market determines, private companies have no market in which to trade.

Consequently, a value known as the Fair Market Value (FMV) must be determined in another way. This will be done annually by an independent chartered business valuator.

An independent valuation of the company will be carried out by [name of firm] as of [date] to determine the FMV of the company.

The independent valuation will derive the FMV using methodologies generally accepted in valuing knowledge-based industries. The primary method of valuation to be used will likely be a capitalization of earnings. Alternate methods such as discounted cash flow analysis, replacement value, and gross revenue multipliers will also be assessed for the company.

The valuator will, among other things, undertake an investigation of the affairs of the company and conduct interviews with certain key officers and larger customers; review historical financial statements and future projections; review certain key contracts; review publicly available information about the industry; and assess the financial performance of companies considered to be similar.

Annual valuations are to be done by an independent business appraiser appointed by the Directors. The valuation date to be used as the initial base value for the ESOP is the fiscal year for the company. The subsequent annual valuation dates will also be at each fiscal year-end. If the fiscal year-end changes, the valuation date will change accordingly. Normally, the valuation update is released approximately three months after year-end, subject to the release of the year-end financial statements.

14. Buyout Conditions

There is no market for the shares other than a buyout by the company, an IPO, or a third-party purchase of the company. However, the ESOP legal advisors will provide details of the technical aspects of a buyout in specific circumstances, which will be presented in full in the Information Package.

To summarize, under the shareholders' agreement (which each employee will be required to sign upon purchasing ESOP shares), shares can be sold back to the company in specific circumstances only. Events that will trigger a buy-back include:

  a. Death of the employee;

  b. Disability of the employee;

c. Bankruptcy of the employee;

d. Termination of the employee;

e. Resignation by the employee;

f. Retirement of the employee; and

g. The employee shares being affected by the employees' separation or divorce.

Employees who leave due to death, disability, or retirement will receive FMV with the applicable minority discount (see Pricing section).

Employees who resign or leave due to termination, or are subject to bankruptcy or Family Law will, in general, receive the lesser of their original cost plus interest (at the average annual Royal Bank prime rate) or FMV with the applicable minority discount.

The compensation committee has the authority to overrule the buy/sell provision in special cases.

15. Pricing

How the Share Value is calculated for a buyout in specific circumstances

Since the ESOP will have a minority of company common shares, it will be considered a minority shareholding. The value of a minority shareholding (such as an ESOP) in a private company is generally at a discount from the total company fair market value. The reason is that the minority interest is illiquid so it cannot realize its value, unlike the majority shareholder who has the ability to sell control of the company.

Studies in Canada and the US have shown that the median discount for a minority shareholding is approximately 30 percent with a range of 10 percent to 50 percent.

For this company, which has a small minority shareholding, a discount of 30 percent will apply. This means that if the total fair market value of the company is $x per share, the purchase or sell price for the employees will be $(x - .3x) per share.

16. Disclosure of Information to Employees

Financial disclosure to employees will be annual sales, gross margin and operating income history (for the past five years + forecasts), and the current balance sheet.

CRITICAL PATH

The ESOP process will follow the time path outlined below:

Weeks 1–3	Set up ESOP advisory team
	Scope ESOP parameters
	Select employee representative(s) for the ESOP team
	Obtain documents for ESOP design and valuation
Week 4	Distribute questionnaire to employees
Week 5	Return questionnaires
Week 6	Start ESOP design
Week 7	Employee announcement to introduce ESOP (optional)
Week 9	Draft valuation
	Distribute draft Employee Blueprint to ESOP team
Week 11	Finalize valuation
Week 12	Finalize Blueprint and start on legal and tax documents
Week 13	Distribute Employee Blueprint to employees
Week 16	Distribute draft legal and tax documents to ESOP team
Week 20	Finalize legal and tax documents
Week 21	Compile Employee Information Package and distribute to employees
Week 22	Town Hall meeting
Week 24	Close ESOP transaction

APPENDIX VI

SHAREHOLDERS' AGREEMENT

made this[ ]day of [   ] ,

B E T W E E N:

Employee Shareholders

-    and –

X TECHNOLOGIES INC., a corporation incorporated pursuant to the laws of the Province of Ontario (the "Corporation")

-    and –

Y CO., a corporation to be amalgamated pursuant to the laws of the Province of Ontario ("Y Co")

WHEREAS pursuant to the Corporation's Employee Share Ownership Plan, Shares may be acquired or options may be issued to Qualifying Employees from time to time to acquire Shares;

AND WHEREAS pursuant to the Plan, one of the conditions imposed on a Qualifying Employee who wishes to acquire Shares is that such Qualifying Employee enter into the herein Shareholder Agreement;

THEREFORE THIS AGREEMENT WITNESSETH that in consideration of the covenants, agreements, and promises herein set forth and other good and valuable consideration (the receipt and sufficiency of which each of the parties hereto acknowledge), the parties agree as follows:

ARTICLE 1.00

DEFINITIONS

In this Agreement, the following definitions will apply:

"*Board*" means the board of directors of the Corporation;

"Business Day" means a day, other than a Saturday, a Sunday or a day which is a statutory holiday in the City of Toronto;

"Corporation" means X Technologies Inc.;

"Control" has the meaning ascribed to it in the Business Corporations Act (Ontario);

"Employee Shareholder" means a Qualifying Employee who has acquired Shares pursuant to the Plan;

"ESOP Offering" means an availment of Shares to Qualifying Employees under the Plan;

"Permanently Disabled" means **[Insert definition from the Corporation's long-term disability group insurance coverage or if no long-term coverage]** the inability of an Employee Shareholder to substantially perform the duties of his or her employment as a result of illness, accident, physical, or mental disability or any other cause, either for a period of six consecutive months or for any 180 days in any 365-day period;

"Plan" means the Corporation's Employee Share Ownership Plan, as the same may be amended from time to time;

"Qualifying Employee" means an employee of the Corporation who has been continuously employed by the Corporation on a full-time basis from no later than October 1, 1999 until January 10, 2000 and, hereafter, includes those employees of the Corporation who have at least six (6) months continuous full-time employment with the Corporation prior to the date of an ESOP Offering;

"Shares" means the Common shares and the Special shares of the Corporation and includes any shares or securities of the Corporation to which such shares are changed, classified, re-classified, subdivided, consolidated, or converted; and

"Share Value" in respect of a Share shall be the most recent fair market values of the Shares determined by the Board in its sole discretion which valuation shall not have occurred more than twelve (12) months prior to the date of determination of Share Value as required hereunder; providing that in making such a determination, the Board may use whatever method or assistance it may deem necessary, including, without limitation, engaging a third party to assist in making such an assessment.

ARTICLE 2.00

PROHIBITION ON TRANSFER OR SALE OF SHARES BY EMPLOYEE SHAREHOLDERS

2.1 Prohibition

No Employee Shareholder shall sell, assign, transfer, encumber, pledge or dispose of his or her shares, except as provided in this Agreement.

ARTICLE 3.00

CHANGES IN CONTROL OF THE CORPORATION

3.1 Drag-Along

If the completion of any contemplated sale of Shares by Y Co. to a third party or third parties (in this section the "*Offeror*") is conditional upon the Offeror acquiring all of the issued Shares of the Corporation, all Employee Shareholders shall be deemed to have granted Y Co. options to purchase all of the Shares held by the Employee Shareholders on the terms and conditions set forth in the offer from the Offeror, which options shall be conditional for the benefit of Y Co. upon the closing of the sale by Y Co. to the Offeror.

3.2 Tag-Along

If the completion of any contemplated sale of Shares by Y Co. to a third party or parties (herein the "*Offeror*") would result in a change of Control of the Corporation, but subject to section 3.1 above, Y Co. has no right to sell any of the Shares held by it unless an offer on identical terms is made to all Employee Shareholders.

3.3 Conditions Precedent to Share Transfer

No share transfer shall be permitted or recorded to a third-party purchaser unless the following conditions are first fulfilled:

(a) The provisions of this section are complied with; and

(b) A true copy of the accepted third party offer between Y Co. and any Offeror under section 3.1 and 3.2 and a statutory declaration of Y Co. and the Offeror that the transaction was completed in accordance with the terms of the Offeror's offer are delivered to each Employee Shareholder and this article applies to any sales created by the "come-along" section set out above.

3.4 Listing of Any of the Shares on a Public Stock Exchange or an Initial Public Offering

In the event that there is a listing of any of the Shares on a public stock exchange and/or there is an initial public offering of any of the Shares, the Employee Shareholders, but subject at all time to any holding requirements insofar as the Shares held by the Employee Shareholders are concerned as may be imposed by such exchange, applicable securities law or the terms of the initial public offering, shall cease to be bound by the provisions of Article 2.00 hereof and Y Co. shall cease to be bound by 3.1, 3.2., and 3.3 hereof.

ARTICLE 4.00

COMPULSORY SALE OF AN EMPLOYEE SHAREHOLDER'S SHARES

4.1 Sale Events

In the event of:

(a) The death of an Employee Shareholder;

(b) The permanent disability of an Employee Shareholder;

(c) The cessation of an Employee Shareholder's employment with the Corporation for any reason whatsoever, including an unlawful termination, provided such cessation occurs no earlier than five (5) years from the date hereof;

(d) The bankruptcy or insolvency of an Employee Shareholder;

(e) The material breach by an Employee Shareholder of the herein Shareholder Agreement or any other agreement an Employee Shareholder has with the Corporation; or

(f) The cessation of an Employee Shareholder's employment with the Corporation for any reason whatsoever, including an unlawful termination, on a date prior to five (5) years from the date hereof (the "Sale Events"),

the provisions of this Article shall apply.

4.2 Agreement of Purchase and Sale

The Corporation shall purchase and the subject Employee Shareholder shall sell all of the Employee Shareholder's Shares.

4.3 Sale Price

4.3.1   If the subject sale of Shares is triggered by the occurrence of one of the Sale Events set out in section 4.1 (a), (b) or (c) above, the purchase price for the Shares shall be the greater of:

(a) The Share Value multiplied by the number of Shares held by the subject Employee Shareholder; and

(b) The cost to the Employee Shareholder of the Shares plus interest at a rate adjusted on the first day of each month to the prime commercial lending rate in effect at the Corporation's primary lending bank on such date per annum calculated monthly from the date of the acquisition of the subject Shares by the Employee Shareholder.

4.3.2   If the subject sale of Shares is triggered by the occurrence of one of the Sale Events set out in section 4.1 (d), (e) or (f) above, the purchase price for the Shares shall be the lesser of:

(a) The Share Value multiplied by the number of Shares held by the subject Employee Shareholder; and

(b) The cost to the Employee Shareholder of the Shares plus interest at a rate adjusted on the first day of each month to the prime commercial lending rate in effect at the Corporation's primary lending bank on such date per annum calculated monthly from the date of the acquisition of the subject Shares by the Employee Shareholder.

4.4 Closing Date

The herein transaction of purchase and sale shall be closed on the 30th day following the occurrence of the Sale Event or if such day is not a Business Day, the transaction shall be closed on the next Business Day following.

4.5 Terms of Payment

The purchase price shall be satisfied on closing as follows:

(i)   By the payment in cash of an amount equal to one-third of the purchase price to the Selling Employee Shareholder; and

(ii)   The delivery to the Selling Employee Shareholder of a promissory note for the balance of the purchase price together with interest providing for payments of one-half of the balance outstanding on the first anniversary of the closing date and the other half on the second anniversary of the closing date together.

ARTICLE 5.00

FORCED TRANSFER

5.1   Events Triggering Option in Favour of Corporation

If, at any time, an application or proceeding under the *Family Law Act (Ontario)*, the *Succession Law Reform Act (Ontario)*, or the *Divorce Act (Canada)* (in each case, as amended or replaced from time to time), or similar legislation in other jurisdictions, is commenced by an Employee Shareholder or his spouse, former spouse, or dependent to determine the entitlement of such spouse, former spouse, or dependent to a payment in respect of an Employee Shareholder's net family property or to support from an Employee Shareholder, such Employee Shareholder shall forthwith give notice to the Corporation of the commencement of such application or proceeding. The Corporation shall have the right (but not the obligation) exercisable on written notice to the Employee Shareholder within ninety (90) days after the delivery of the Notice, to purchase all of the Shares owned by such Employee Shareholder.

5.2 Agreement of Purchase and Sale

If the Option is exercised, the Corporation shall purchase and the subject Employee Shareholder shall sell all of the Employee Shareholder's Shares.

5.3 Sale Price

The purchase price for the Shares shall be the lesser of:

(a) The Share Value multiplied by the number of Shares held by the subject Employee Shareholder; and

(b) The cost to the Employee Shareholder of the Shares plus interest at a rate adjusted on the first day of each month to the prime commercial lending rate in effect at the Corporation's primary lending bank on such date per annum calculated monthly from the date of the acquisition of the subject Shares by the Employee Shareholder.

5.4 Closing Date

The transaction shall be closed on the 30th day following the exercise of the aforesaid Option or if such day is not a Business Day, the transaction shall be closed on the next Business Day following.

5.5 Terms of Payment

The purchase price shall be satisfied on closing as follows:

(i) By the payment in cash of an amount equal to one-third of the purchase price to the Selling Employee Shareholder; and

(ii) The delivery to the Selling Employee Shareholder of a promissory note for the balance of the purchase price together with interest providing for payments of one-half of the balance outstanding on the first anniversary of the closing date and the other half on the second anniversary of the closing date together.

ARTICLE 6.00

TERMS OF SALE

6.1 **Application**

The provisions of this Article apply to any sale by an Employee Shareholder to the Corporation of any of an Employee Shareholder's Shares pursuant to a provision hereof including section 3.1. The specific terms of any such section or article of this agreement shall prevail over the provisions hereof in the event of conflict.

6.2 **Time and Place for Closing**

The closing of the transaction shall take place at the office of the principal place of business of the Corporation at 2 o'clock in the afternoon on the date fixed for closing.

6.3 **Documents from Selling Employee Shareholder on Closing**

The Selling Employee Shareholder shall deliver the following:

(a) A release to Y Co. and to the Corporation from the provisions of this agreement save as to those provisions specifically stated to continue after termination of this agreement;

(b) All certificates representing the Shares that are being transferred, duly endorsed to the Corporation and appointing the Corporation the subject Employee Shareholder's attorney to transfer such Shares on the records of the Corporation;

(c) An undertaking to give such further assurances and do all other things as may be necessary in order to deliver title to the Shares free and clear of the claims of all others; and

(d) A covenant that the Selling Employee Shareholder is the owner with good and marketable title, free of any encumbrances and liens of any kind of the Shares, and that the Selling Shareholder has the exclusive right and power to sell, transfer, and assign the Shares to the Corporation.

6.4 Documents from the Corporation

On closing the Corporation will deliver to the Selling Employee Shareholder the following:

(a) The monies due the Selling Employee Shareholder on closing;

(b) The promissory note as provided for in this Agreement as payment for the balance of the purchase price; and

(c) A release from this agreement except those provisions hereof as provided will survive the termination of this agreement.

6.5 Default in Payment

If the Corporation shall default in payment of principal or interest due on any deferred balance of the purchase price or default in the performance of any covenant given by it, and such default shall continue for a period of fifteen (15) days after written notice is given by the Selling Employee Shareholder, without prejudice to any other rights which the Selling Employee Shareholder may have, the whole unpaid balance of the purchase price shall, at the option of the Selling Employee Shareholder, immediately become due and payable in full.

6.6 Set-off Rights

The Corporation shall have the right to set off against any sums of money due the Selling Employee Shareholder the amount of any indebtedness of the Selling Employee Shareholder to the Corporation, notwithstanding that such indebtedness shall not then have been matured and be due and payable.

6.7 Appointment of Attorney

The Selling Employee Shareholder hereby irrevocably appoints each and every one of the Corporation, each director thereof and the Corporation's President the Selling Employee Shareholder's attorney for the purposes of this section. Such appointment and power of attorney, being coupled with an interest, shall not be revoked by the insolvency, bankruptcy, death or incapacity of the Selling Employee Shareholder and the Selling Employee Shareholder hereby ratifies and confirms all that the Selling Employee Shareholder's attorneys may lawfully do or cause to be done by virtue of such power of attorney. If the Selling Employee Shareholder shall neglect or refuse at attend at closing and deliver the transfers, instruments, and other documents provided herein, the attorney is authorized to execute and deliver all such transfers, instruments, and other documents on behalf of an in the name of the Selling Employee Shareholder. The attorney shall forthwith thereafter deliver to the Selling Employee Shareholder true copies of all such transfers, instruments, and documents as executed.

6.8 Tendering

Tendering of money shall be sufficient if made by accepted cheque or bank draft drawn on a Canadian chartered bank, and any tender may be made upon the parties.

ARTICLE 7.00

MICRO MARKET

7.1 Commencing October 1, 2004 and each October 1st thereafter (or if October 1st is not a Business Day the next Business Day thereafter) at 10 a.m. at the Corporation's head office, an auction will take place (the "*Auction*").

7.2 The items to be auctioned at the Auctions shall be those of the Corporation's issued Common shares held by those of the Employee Shareholders who submit Asks as hereinafter contemplated.

7.3 The Auctions shall be conducted under the following terms:

(a) The Corporation's President shall appoint an auctioneer for the subject Auction (the "Auctioneer").

(b) Each Employee Shareholder shall be entitled to offer at the Auction at least 100 of his Common shares, up to a maximum of 20 percent of his then current Common shareholdings and each such offer shall specify a minimum price per share that that Employee Shareholder would accept for the Common shares that he or she is offering (an "Ask").

(c) All Asks shall be in writing on a form to be prepared by the Auctioneer, shall be signed by the Employee Shareholder submitting the Ask and shall contain the following information only:

(i) The number of the Employee Shareholder's Common shares available; and

(ii) The minimum price per share that that Employee Shareholder is prepared to accept.

(d) At 10 a.m. on the day scheduled for the Auction, the Auctioneer shall make available to those Employee Shareholders who request same at that time, the form to be used to submit an Ask.

(e) An Ask shall not be deemed to have been made unless it is in the hands of the Auctioneer no later that 10:15 a.m. on the day scheduled for the Auction and shall not be deemed valid until the Auctioneer declares that it complies with this agreement.

(f) The order of the auction of the valid Asks shall be determined by lot, in the Auctioneer's absolute discretion, and once determined shall be followed.

(g) Each Ask in turn will be auctioned by the Auctioneer.

(h) All bids for each Ask as presented shall be for the entire subject matter of the Ask and shall be in writing on a bid form to be made available by the Auctioneer and signed by the Employee Shareholder submitting the bid. Nothing shall be added to the bid form except the amount per share of the bid and the signature of the Employee Shareholder submitting the bid. The bid shall not be deemed to have been made until it is in the hands of the Auctioneer and shall not be deemed to be valid until the Auctioneer declares that it complies with this agreement and, as such, is valid and announces to all present the amount of it.

(i) Subject to the minimum Ask price as alluded to above, the initial bid may be in any amount. Each subsequent bid shall be made within one minute of the immediately preceding announced bid and the amount of each successive bid shall be greater than the immediately preceding bid by an amount of not less than five percent of the previous bid.

(j) The bidding shall be deemed to have been terminated if more than one minute elapses during which time no valid bid has been made, in which case the last bid shall be deemed to comprise a valid offer, by the Employee Shareholder who submitted it, to purchase the subject matter of the Ask from the Employee Shareholder who submitted same for a price per share equal to the amount of the last bid and the other Employee Shareholder shall be deemed to have accepted such offer and an agreement of purchase and sale shall be deemed to have been created between them.

(k) In regard to any dispute or disagreement arising respecting any matter pertaining to the Auction or to the conduct thereof, the determination by the Auctioneer with respect thereto shall be final and binding on all Employee Shareholders and there shall be no appeal or review therefrom.

(l) The fees of the Auctioneer shall be borne by the Corporation.

(m) Any agreement of purchase and sale created pursuant to the provisions above, shall be completed on the seventh day following the Auction date. At that time, the purchase price will be paid in cash or by certified cheque or bank draft by the purchaser and the seller shall transfer and deliver to the purchaser good and marketable title to the subject Common shares free and clear of all encumbrances and deliver to the buyer a duly completed certificate.

ARTICLE 8.00

GENERAL

8.1 **Share Certificates**

All outstanding certificates representing any of the Shares shall have endorsed thereon a notation to the effect that the shares represented by such certificate are subject to the terms of this Agreement. Further, all such share certificates shall be held for safekeeping by the Corporation.

8.2 **Termination**

This Agreement shall continue in force until the earlier of:

(a) in respect of any Employee Shareholder, on the date such Employee Shareholder ceases to hold any Shares governed by this Agreement;

(b) the date on which the Corporation is dissolved in accordance with the applicable provisions of the Business Corporations Act (Ontario); and

(c) the Shares of the Corporation are listed on a public stock exchange.

8.3 Notice

Any notice or document required to be given to an Employee Shareholder, Y Co., or the Corporation shall be in writing and if sent by courier shall be deemed to have been given on the second Business Day after delivery to the courier for dispatch. Notice transmitted by a form of recorded communication shall be deemed given on the first Business Day after transmission. Any party may from time to time notify the others in the manner provided herein of any change of address which thereafter, until changed by like notice, shall be the address of such party for all purposes hereof.

8.4 Entire Agreement

This Agreement sets forth the entire agreement among the parties hereto pertaining to the subject matter hereof and supersedes all prior agreements, understandings, negotiations, and discussions, whether oral or written, between the parties hereto, and there are no warranties, representations, and other agreements between the parties hereto in connection with the subject matter hereof except as specifically set forth herein. No supplement, modification, waiver, or termination of this agreement shall be binding unless executed in writing by the parties to be bound thereby. No waiver of any of the provisions of this Agreement shall be deemed or shall constitute a waiver of any other provision nor shall such waiver constitute a continuing waiver unless otherwise expressly provided. This agreement shall be binding upon the parties hereto and their respective heirs, executors, successors, and permitted assigns.

8.5 Severability

If in any jurisdiction, any provision of this Agreement or its application to any party or circumstance is restricted, prohibited, or unenforceable, such provision shall, as to such jurisdiction, be ineffective only to the extent of such restriction, prohibition, or unenforceability without invalidating the remaining provisions hereof and without affecting the validity or enforceability of such provision in any other jurisdiction or its application to other parties or circumstances.

8.6 Independent Legal Advice

Each Employee Shareholder hereby acknowledges having been advised to obtain independent legal representation or advice, prior to executing this Agreement and thereby becoming bound by its terms and subject to its obligations. Further, each Employee Shareholder acknowledges that the herein Agreement has been prepared for and on behalf of the Corporation by the Corporation's solicitors who do not represent the Employee Shareholders or any of them.

8.7 Governing Law

This Agreement shall be governed and construed in accordance with the laws of the Province of Ontario.

8.8 Employee Share Ownership Plan

Each Employee Shareholder agrees and acknowledges that the provisions hereof relate only to Shares acquired pursuant to the Plan. Each Employee Shareholder further agrees and acknowledges that Shares otherwise acquired by an Employee Shareholder will be governed by other agreements.

8.9 Assignment

Except as otherwise permitted under this Agreement, the interest of any Employee Shareholder hereunder shall not be assigned to any person without the consent in writing of all of the other parties hereto.

8.10 Time of Essence

Time shall in all respects be of the essence of this Agreement.

8.11 Severability

In the event that any provision in any article or section of this agreement is held to be invalid or unenforceable by a court of competent jurisdiction, such invalidity or unenforceability shall not affect the remainder of the provisions hereof, but such part shall be fully sever-able and this agreement shall be construed and enforced as if such arti-cle or section had never been included herein.

8.12 Enurement

This agreement shall enure to the benefit of and be binding upon the parties and their respective heirs, executors, administrators, suc-cessors, and assigns, as the case may be.

Y CO.

Per: _____
              Authorized Signing Officer
I have authority to bind the Corporation.
X TECHNOLOGIES INC.

Per: _____
              Authorized Signing Officer
I have authority to bind the Corporation.

APPENDIX VII

SOURCES: WEB SITES AND MORE

Employee Ownership Report. A 16-page bimonthly newsletter of The National Center for Employee Ownership (NCEO). Contains news on legal, regulatory, and financial developments; ideas, tips, and reports on management practices in employee ownership firms; technical articles by employee ownership experts; research and case studies; a one-page pullout for rank-and-file employees; and company, media, and resource information.

   Contact: 1736 Franklin St., 8th Floor,
                     Oakland, CA 94612
                     Telephone: (510) 208-1300
                     Fax: (510) 272-9510
   Web site: http://www.nceo.org/

The ESOP Report. Published 11 times per year by The ESOP Association, it covers the latest regulatory and case law updates, Capitol Hill briefings, technical and managerial advice from ESOP professionals, tips on winning ESOP companies and employee owners, and association news.

   Contact: 1726 M Street, NW, Suite 501,
                     Washington, DC 20036
                     Telephone: (202) 293-2971
                     Fax: (202) 293-7568
   Web site: www.esopassociation.org

Frederic W. Cook & Co., Inc. The 2000 Top 250 *Long-Term and Stock-Based Grant Practices for Executives and Directors.* Web site also includes latest Alert Letters and Industry News.

   Web site: www.fredericwcook.com

Hay Group, Inc. *The Hay Report* is an annual strategic update that examines the state of compensation practices.

                     Telephone: (781) 239-1111
   Web site: www.haygroup.com

Hewitt Associates. A global management consulting firm specializing in human resource solutions. Compensation surveys, research papers, and other publications are available on their web site.

Web site: www.hewitt.com

Participate! The Employee Ownership & Incentives Association (EOIA) Newsletter.

Contact: 548 Beatty St.,
Vancouver, BC, Canada, V6B 2L3
Telephone: (604) 687-3767 or toll-free at (877) 687-3767
Fax: (604) 687-3770
Web site: www.esopcanada.org

PricewaterhouseCoopers Incentive Stock Plans Worldwide Reporter. A web-based subscription service detailing the tax, legal, and administrative issues of offering stock incentives in 71 countries.

Contact: (650) 853-8380
Web site: www.pwcglobal.com

The ESOP Association (Canada).

Contact: 390 Bay St., Suite 2000,
Toronto, Ontario, M5H 2Y2
ESOP Insights Newsletter
Telephone: (416) 862-2345
Fax: (604) 687-3770
Web site: www.esop-canada.com

Towers Perrin Monitor. A monthly newsletter covering key developments and trends in the United States published by the global management consultant company.

Web site: www.towersperrin.com

Towers Perrin Monitor-Update. A bulletin published occasionally to provide employers with information and analysis of major legal and regulatory developments affecting benefit strategies.

Web site: www.towersperrin.com

WestWard Pay Strategies. Consultants specializing in executive, incentive, and stock compensation issues. Web site includes several studies of stock compensation practices in high-tech companies.

    Contact: 850 Montgomery Street, Suite 250,
                San Francisco, CA 94133
                Telephone: (415) 217-8200
                Fax: (415) 217-8201
    Web site: www.westwardpay.com

workspan (formerly ACA News). Periodical published by WorldatWork, The Professional Association for Compensation, Benefits and Total Rewards (formerly American Compensation Association).

                Customer Relations:
                (877) 951-9191 or
                in Canada (905) 893-1689
    Web site: www.worldatwork.org

WorldatWork Journal (formerly ACA Journal). Periodical published by WorldatWork, The Professional Association for Compensation, Benefits, and Total Rewards (formerly American Compensation Association)

                Customer Relations:
                (877) 951-9191 or
                in Canada (905) 893-1689
    Web site: www.worldatwork.org

APPENDIX VIII

INSTITUTIONS

Australian Employee Ownership Association (AEOA). A non-profit, non-political association promoting the benefits of employee ownership.

Contact: GPO Box 2649,
Sydney 2001
Telephone: (+612) 9299 2829
Fax: (+612) 9299 1991
Web site: www.aeoa.org.au

The Employee Ownership & Incentives Association (EOIA). A non-profit research and education organization dedicated to fostering the growth and development of broad-based employee ownership and incentives, employee share purchase plans, stock options, and employee involvement. Web site includes research articles and case studies.

Contact: 548 Beatty St.,
Vancouver, BC, Canada, V6B 2L3
Telephone: (604) 687-3767 or toll-free at (877) 687-3767
Fax: (604) 687-3770
Web site: www.esopcanada.org

The Employee Share Ownership Centre. A non-profit subscription-based organization founded to inform, lobby, and research in the interest of developing all forms of broad-based employee share ownership plans in the UK and Europe.

Contact: 2 Ridgmount Street,
London WC1E 7AA
Telephone: (44) 020 7436 9936
Fax: (44) 020 7580 0016
Web site: www.mhcc.co.uk/esop

ESOP ASSOCIATION CANADA. A non-profit organization founded for the purpose of promoting the concept of employee ownership for business in Canada.

Contact: 390 Bay St., Suite 2000,
            Toronto, Ontario, M5H 2Y2
            Telephone: (416) 862-2345
            Fax: (416) 749-1969
Web site: www.esop-canada.com

The ESOP Association. A national, non-profit association in the US dedicated to employee ownership with a focus on ESOPs and employee ownership.

Contact: 1726 M Street, NW, Suite 501,
            Washington, DC 20036
            Telephone: (202) 293-2971
            Fax: (202) 293-7568
Web site: www.esopassociation.org

European Federation of Employed Shareholders (EFES). Developing a European centre for information, meeting, training, advice, representation, and lobbying to serve its members. EFES also organizes many events and meetings in Europe to promote and develop the participation of employee owners.

Contact: Marc Mathieu,
            Avenue Voltaire 135 - B-1030 Brussels
            Fax: 32(0) 2 242 64 30
            E-mail: marc.mathieu@ping.be
Web site: www.ping.be/fas/

The Financial Accounting Standards Board. Establishes and improves standards of financial accounting and reporting for the guidance and education of the public, including issuers, auditors, and users of financial information.

Contact: 401 Merritt 7, P.O. Box 5116,
            Norwalk, Connecticut 06856-5116
            Telephone: (203) 847-0700 or (800) 748-0659
            Fax: (203) 849-9714
Web site: www.fasb.org

The Foundation for Enterprise Development. A non-profit organization dedicated to helping entrepreneurs and executives use employee ownership and equity compensation as a fair and effective means of motivating the work force and improving corporate performance. Web site includes an online employee ownership magazine and a resource library.

Web site: www.fed.org

International Foundation of Employee Benefit Plans (IFEBP). A non-profit, non-lobbying, educational association serving the employee benefits field. Web site includes industry news and a listing of publications.

Contact: 18700 W. Bluemound Rd., P.O. Box 69,
            Brookfield, WI 53008-0069
            Telephone: (262) 786-6700
            Fax: (262) 786-8670
            Instant Information Fax Service: (888) 217-5960
Web site: www.ifebp.org

The National Association of Stock Plan Professionals. Provides opportunities for education, networking, and information exchange through its national office, local chapters, and national and local conferences. Members are professionals whose responsibilities are related, directly or indirectly, to stock plan administration and design.

Contact: P.O. Box 21639, Concord, CA 94521-0639
            Telephone: (925) 685-9271
            Fax: (925) 685-5402
Web site: www.naspp.com

The National Center for Employee Ownership (NCEO). A private, non-profit membership and research organization that serves as a source of unbiased information on employee stock ownership plans (ESOPs), broadly granted employee stock options, and employee participation programs. Web site includes publications on ESOPs, stock options, and participation.

Contact: 1736 Franklin St., 8th Floor, Oakland, CA 94612
            Telephone: (510) 208-1300
            Fax: (510) 272-9510
Web site: http://www.nceo.org/

Ohio Employee Ownership Center (OEOC). A non-profit, university-based program established to provide outreach, information, and preliminary technical assistance to Ohio employees and business owners interested in exploring employee ownership.

  Contact: Kent State University, P.O. Box 5190
              309 Franklin Hall, Kent, OH 44242-0001
              Telephone: (330) 672-3028
              Fax: (330) 672-4063
Web site: http://dept.kent.edu/oeoc/

WorldatWork. The Professional Association for Compensation, Benefits, and Total Rewards. (Formerly American Compensation Association)

              Customer Relations: (877) 951-9191 or
              in Canada (905) 893-1689
Web site: www.worldatwork.org

APPENDIX IX

Want to keep up-to-date with ESOPs? If so, please forward your name, title, email address, and corporate name to ESOP Builders Inc. ESOP Builders Inc. will send you their monthly ESOP newsletter by email. No solicitation will be forthcoming through this update, nor will your name be put on any mailing list.

A LIST OF ESOP PROFESSIONALS

ESOP design

ESOP Builders Inc.
> www.esopbuilders.com
> (905) 625-8118

Contact: Ian McDowell x 233
> ian@esopbuilders.com
> Perry Phillips x 228
> perry@esopbuilders.com
> Suite 420, 2560 Matheson Blvd East
> Mississauga, Ontario L4W 4Y9

William Mercer
Contact: Bonnie Flatt, Principal
> bonnie.flatt@ca.wmmercer.com
> (416) 868-2857
> BCE Place, 161 Bay Street, PO Box 501
> Toronto, Ontario M5J 2S5

Cross-border ESOPs

ESOP Builders Inc.
> www.esopbuilders.com
> (905) 625-8118
Contact: Ian McDowell x 233

ian@esopbuilders.com
Perry Phillips x 228
perry@esopbuilders.com
Suite 420, 2560 Matheson Blvd East
Mississauga, Ontario L4W 4Y9

National Benefit Services Inc.

(312) 372-2150 Fax
(312) 372-7673
Assisting employers since the early 1980s with design, administration, and communication of their ESOPs and stock options. Employee ownership specialist for overseas enterprise development projects sponsored by the US Agency for International Development.

Contact: Jerry Kalish jerry@nationalbenefit.com
309 W. Washington Street, Suite 1250
Chicago, Illinois 60606 USA

Business valuation

Canadian Institute of Chartered Business Valuators

www.businessvaluators.com
Maintains registry of members
(416) 204-3396
277 Wellington Street West
Toronto, Ontario M5V 3H2

Phillips Valuations Inc.

(416) 861-0024

Contact: Perry Phillips CA CBV ASA
philvalu@fox.nstn.ca
390 Bay Street, Suite 2000
Toronto, Ontario M5H 2Y2

Law firms

Baker Mackenzie

www.bakerinfo.com/toronto

Stock-based compensation plans and international compensation issues.

Contact: Adam Balinsky
adam.balinsky@bakernet.com
(416) 865-6962
Victoria Stewart
victoria.a.stewart@bakernet.com (San Francisco)
(415) 576-3000
BCE Place, 181 Bay Street, Suite 2100/P.O. Box 874
Toronto, Ontario M5J 2T3

Lafleur Brown

(416) 869-0994
Contact: Steve Alizadeh
salizadeh@lbcan.com
(416) 869-8400
National Bank Building 150 York Street, 14th floor
Toronto, Ontario M5H 3E5

Lawrence Lawrence Stevenson

(905) 451-3040
Contact: William Sirdevan
wsirde@lawrences.com
43 Queen St. West,
Brampton, Ontario L6Y 1L9

Koskie Minsky

(416) 977-8353
Contact: George Dzuro
ext. 282
gdzuro@koskieminsky.com
20 Queen Street West,
Suite 900, Box 52,
Toronto, Ontario M5H 3R3

Wilson Vukelich

www.wilsonvukelich.com
(905) 940-8700
Contact: Jordan Dolgin

jdolgin@wilsonvukelich.com
60 Columbia Way, Suite 710,
Markham, Ontario L3R 0C9

Tax accountants

Canadian Institute of Chartered Accountants (CICA)
(416) 977-3222
277 Wellington Street West,
Toronto, Ontario M5V 3H2
Each province has its own institute which maintains a registry of members by specialty.

Institute of Chartered Accountants of Ontario (ICAO)
(416) 962-1841
69 Bloor Street East
Toronto

Vottero Fremes McGrath Yee
(905) 625-5688
Contact: Michael Fremes
mjfremes@vfmy.com x 223
Suite 420, 2560 Matheson Blvd East
Mississauga, Ontario L4W 4Y9

Open-book management

Rooney Greig, Inc.
(514) 421-3955
Fax (514) 421-1383
A team of professionals, predominantly Chartered Accountants, dedicated to the success of their clients, will assist in implementing tools such as open-book management allowing owners and managers to improve their businesses.
Contact: Danny Greig
dannyg@rgwf.com
1255, Transcanadienne, #320
Dorval, Quebec H9P 2V4

Profit-sharing

Tyson & Associates Limited

         http://www.compensationcanada.com

         (416) 966-1379

         Fax (416) 966-8715

         Management consultants specializing in compensation, including profit sharing.

Contact: David E. Tyson

         tyson.consult@sympatico.ca

         Suite 210, 83 Elm Avenue

         Toronto, Ontario M4W 1P1